SCHO
THE WORL
REPRES

Continuum *Reader's Guides*

Continuum's *Reader's Guides* are clear, concise and accessible introductions to classic works of philosophy. Each book explores the major themes, historical and philosophical context and key passages of a major philosophical text, guiding the reader toward a thorough understanding of often demanding material. Ideal for undergraduate students, the guides provide an essential resource for anyone who needs to get to grips with a philosophical text.

Reader's Guides available from Continuum

SCHOPENHAUER'S
THE WORLD AS WILL AND REPRESENTATION

A Reader's Guide

ROBERT WICKS

continuum

Continuum International Publishing Group

The Tower Building	80 Maiden Lane
11 York Road	Suite 704
London SE1 7NX	New York, NY 10038

www.continuumbooks.com

British Library Cataloguing-in-Publication Data
A catalogue record for this book is available from the British Library.

ISBN: HB: 978-1-4411-3785-2
PB: 978-1-4411-0434-2

Library of Congress Cataloging-in-Publication Data
Wicks, Robert, 1954-
Schopenhauer's The world as will and representation:
a reader's guide / Robert Wicks.
p. cm.
Includes bibliographical references (p.) and index.
ISBN: 978-1-4411-3785-2 – ISBN: 978-1-4411-0434-2
1. Schopenhauer, Arthur, 1788–1860. Welt als Wille und
Vorstellung. 2. Philosophy. I. Title.

B3139.W53 2011
193–dc22
2010032087

Typeset by Newgen Imaging Systems Pvt Ltd, Chennai, India
Printed and bound in India by Replika Press Pvt Ltd

Ihm ist kein Leiden mehr fremd. (§68)

CONTENTS

ACKNOWLEDGMENTS

This book is dedicated to my students at the University of Auckland over the years, who have attended my classes on Schopenhauer's philosophy. A more maturely attentive, curious, and considerate group of students is difficult to imagine, and I would like to acknowledge my good fortune and gratitude in having had so many occasions to communicate Schopenhauer's ideas to such a fine group of people. Among them are Ella Burton, Yuri Cath, Chris Chetland, Navi Chou, Stephanie Collins, Sam Gavin, Rajasekhar Govindamenon, Aness Kim, Sean Kinsler, 'Aisea Māhina, Scott McBride, Thomas McGuire, Sophie Milne, Harrison Mitchell, Emmet Parker, Justyn Pilbrow, Jordan Reyne, Geoff Roche, Chen Shen, Steve Shen, Hohepa te Pūru/Joseph J. W. Stewart, Rilind Tairi, David Titheridge, Saffron Toms, Andrew Trigg, Craig Wattam, Myles Webster, Daniel Wilson, Brignall Wood, Anatasha Vance, and Benjamin Young.

I would also like to dedicate this book to the memory of one of my teachers, not of Schopenhauer, but of life, and not simply of life in the sense of the biological sciences that he taught so inspirationally, but of life in the sense of what makes life worth living. This is to Howard E. Crouch (1918–2007), founder of the Damien-Dutton Society for Leprosy Aid.

Father Damien (1840–89), who lived and died at the leper colony on the Hawaiian island of Molokai, was the epitome of selflessness and compassion, and it is appropriate to celebrate them both here within the context of Schopenhauer's moral philosophy.

Finally, I would like to thank Ivan Soll, a friend and teacher for the past 30 years, who inspired not only this writer, but many others, to devote their scholarly energies to keeping Schopenhauer philosophically alive and influential.

Auckland, New Zealand
July 4, 2010

CHAPTER 1

CONTEXT

Arthur Schopenhauer (1788–1860) published his main work, *The World as Will and Representation*, in 1818 at the age of 30, convinced that he had developed the outlooks of Plato and Kant—two of the most towering figures in Western philosophy— to a level of consistency never before attained. Readers of Schopenhauer might thus be tempted to refer to him as either a "Platonist" or "Kantian." Although some regard him in this way, it would misrepresent the tenor of his outlook, for the innovations Schopenhauer introduces into Plato's and Kant's views are so radical, that both would have regarded his resulting picture of the world as fundamentally incongruent with their own, far less repentance-oriented visions.

Plato believes that everything rests rationally upon a set of timeless conceptual forms, the highest of which is the form of the Good. These forms are ideal types such as perfect circularity, triangularity, sphericality, justice, courage, piety, and beauty, all of which are conceived to stand as the patterns that inform our daily world, and against which the world's changing objects and events are measured. With a comparably favorable view of the world's foundation, Kant postulates as a moral certainty, a timeless, benevolent, supreme intelligence behind the natural scenes.

Hardly as optimistic, Schopenhauer argues that the universe's core is nothing but a blind, timeless, pointless urge. The most appropriate word he can propose to describe this reality is "Will," as when we speak of "raw" or "sheer" willpower, with nothing but force behind it. He also crucially describes Will as a "lack," as when we feel unfulfilled and hungry for "something more," while yet having no idea of what that something might be. Feelings of empty frustration and indeterminate yearning provide an apt model for Schopenhauer's conception of the universe, if we introduce analogies from human emotion. What drives everything, though, is in itself more severe: Will is unconscious, uncaring, unknowing, amoral, and fundamentally goalless.

For someone like Schopenhauer, who was born into materially privileged circumstances, and who never suffered from the lack of money, education, culture, travel experience, or professional opportunities, this is an unexpectedly unsmiling metaphysics. His father, Heinrich Floris Schopenhauer—up until his death in April 1805, barely two months after Arthur's seventeenth birthday—was a wealthy merchant and ship owner, based in the seaports of Danzig and Hamburg, who prepared his son well for a career in international commerce. Arthur's mother, Johanna Trosiener Schopenhauer, the daughter of a well-established Danzig family, was endowed with a fine intellect, social talents, and impressive abilities as a writer. Despite such an advantageous parentage and cultural surroundings—and in this respect he compares well with Prince Siddhartha Gautama, the Buddha— Schopenhauer grew to appreciate the spiritual impoverishment that comfortable material surroundings can bring about.

After his father died, Schopenhauer faithfully continued his commercial training for two more years, but with his mother's blessing he set aside his future as a businessman to devote his time to scholarly pursuits. At age 21, he entered the University of Göttingen, majoring first in medicine and then in philosophy. This is where he encountered the philosophies of Plato and Kant, and where he studied a variety of subjects that included physics, astronomy, chemistry, botany, anatomy, physiology, psychology, ethnography, and history. Throughout his life, Schopenhauer retained his interest in the sciences.

Schopenhauer's philosophy professor in Göttingen was Gottlob Ernst Schulze (1761–1833), whose place in the German philosophical tradition reveals the academic context within which Schopenhauer entered into his studies. Schulze is known for having recommended to Schopenhauer that the best philosophical grounding is through the careful study of Plato and Kant, and Schopenhauer followed his advice wholeheartedly. Schulze himself worked within a tradition of post-Kantian writers who were reacting to Kant's influential and controversial *Critique of Pure Reason* (1781/87). Some were reformulating Kant's main arguments to preserve and strengthen the theory, as was Karl Leonhard Reinhold (1757–1823); others were trying to refute these respectful reformulations, as was Schulze; still others were developing new philosophical frontiers beyond Kant's conclusions, as were the leading German Idealist philosophers, Johann Gottlieb Fichte (1762–1814), Friedrich Wilhelm Joseph Schelling (1775–1854), and Georg Wilhelm Friedrich Hegel (1770–1831). Schopenhauer would soon number among those who were imaginatively expanding Kant's philosophy, despite how he later repudiated Fichte's, Schelling's, and Hegel's optimism, and how he considered himself merely to be developing and strengthening Kant's main insights.

Within this Kantian intellectual culture, Schulze is a skeptic who challenges one of the leading rational reconstructors of Kant's philosopher, namely, Reinhold, and who advances criticisms against Kant's conception of the world's foundation, the "thing-in-itself." Having absorbed Schulze's arguments—ones that serve as the springboard for Schopenhauer's own departure from Kant—he reiterates them in the substantial appendix to *The World as Will and Representation* entitled, "Criticism of the Kantian Philosophy."

In 1811, Schopenhauer left Göttingen for Berlin to attend Fichte's lectures, who, as the leading philosopher of the day, held the first chair of philosophy at the University of Berlin. The conscientiousness Schopenhauer adopted toward his courses was remarkable, for he recorded Fichte's lectures in his notebooks almost verbatim, doing his best to appreciate the great philosopher's message. This honest effort on Schopenhauer's part ended in disillusionment.

Fichte envisions the universe as a magnificent thought-process constituted by the activity of a rational will—a will whose never-ending reflection and consequent self-enhancement constitutes an ever-increasing advance toward a coherent, thoroughly integrated, moral world, or virtual heaven-on-earth. Fichte's arguments in support of this philosophical vision failed to impress Schopenhauer, partly owing to their impenetrable obscurity. Neither did it help that Fichte's inherent optimism cut squarely against Schopenhauer's psychological grain. We nonetheless have as a product of Schopenhauer's scholarly efforts at ages 23–24, approximately 200 pages—a short book in itself—of Fichte's transcribed lectures from 1811 to 1812.

Schopenhauer eventually abandoned these lectures, convinced that Fichte's general philosophical style—one based on a logic of opposition and reconciliation (or, as Fichte described it, "thesis, antithesis, and synthesis") that Schelling and Hegel fruitfully modified and developed—was fundamentally wrong-headed. As a measure of Schopenhauer's disagreement with this dialectical style, not to mention a distaste for the quasi-theistic outlook he perceived hiding within it, we can note that in his later writings, Schopenhauer ridicules these philosophers with terms such as "windbag," "charlatan," "humbug," and "scribbler." His philosophical reasons reside in the atheistic position he develops in his doctoral dissertation of 1813, entitled *The Fourfold Root of the Principle of Sufficient Reason*, written in the wake of his disappointing experiences in Fichte's classroom.

Owing to their shared belief that the universe is a thought-process whose essence is to become ever more self-conscious and rational, the German Idealist philosophers are associated with pantheism, namely, the idea that "all is God." Since, by their lights, the present generation now spearheads the universe's dramatic journey toward full self-consciousness, they commonly hold that God (i.e., the world) has not yet fully materialized and recognized itself, and that although the world has developed from the days when it was a lifeless mass of minerals and gases, the social-political heaven-on-earth is yet to come. This vision of the divine is sophisticated, extraordinary, attractive, and controversial in its earthly humanism, but Fichte, Schelling, and Hegel can nonetheless be appreciated as attempting to preserve theistic sentiments, despite how their respective conceptions of God depart significantly from the traditional notion of an all-knowing, all-powerful, and all-good personal being located beyond space and time.

In opposition, Schopenhauer expresses an atheistic philosophy in *The World as Will and Representation*, spiced with mysticism. Since he finished the book in 1818 and was attending Fichte's lectures enthusiastically six years earlier, we can form a picture of Schopenhauer's intellectual development by asking when, exactly, Schopenhauer became an atheist. It is interesting to see that his private notebooks contain some theistic sympathies from the years 1808–13, as he theorizes in reference to the concept of God, acknowledges it, and accepts its symbolic use.[1]

When reflecting back upon his youth from a standpoint 20 years later, Schopenhauer recalls that at age 17—this was in 1805, before he attended the university—he, like the Buddha, was distressed by life's misery and wretchedness. The experience supposedly convinced him then, that this world could only be the work of a cruel, gloating devil, rather than an infinitely good deity.[2] From the perspective of the 44-year-old Schopenhauer, he had some impressive atheistic moments during his days as a teenager, although his early notebook entries suggest that he retained some sort of belief in God during the years immediately following, at least until 1813. These details are worth noting because Schopenhauer's mature philosophy conveys mixed sentiments of this very kind. He denies that God exists, but his philosophy never goes so far as to deny that traditional morality is misguided as well. He states that the core of world is Will, but allows also that mystical, liberating states that can arise when we minimize Will's pressure.

Anticipating an attack on the city by Napoleon's troops, Schopenhauer left Berlin in May 1813. After briefly visiting his mother in Weimar, he moved in June to the small, nearby hamlet of Rudolstadt to write his doctoral dissertation over the next three months. This dissertation examined four different forms of necessary connection, all of which were defined relative to the human intellect, and his study implied that questions such as whether God exists are beyond logical proof and standard philosophical treatment. Schopenhauer did not discuss God in the dissertation's first edition, but in the second edition of 1847, he added pointedly that the concept of an "absolutely necessary being" is contradictory. This suggests that by mid-1813, when the first edition was published, his atheism had become well-entrenched.

After completing his dissertation and moving back to Weimar, Schopenhauer became acquainted with philosophical-religious works from India at the very end of 1813 and beginning of 1814. Judging from the Weimar library's records of the books Schopenhauer borrowed, he first read the *Bhagavadgita* in December of 1813 and the *Upanishads* a few months later, in March 1814.[3] These texts impressed Schopenhauer indelibly, for he encountered there a kindred spirit, consistent with the views he had developed independently in his dissertation. Since Indian religion was considered at the time to be among the oldest and most profound in the world, upon discovering his own views implicit in the Indian religious literature, Schopenhauer was convinced that with this authoritative and unexpected support, his own philosophical vision was surely in contact with the truth. His philosophy also provided a much clearer and logically cleaner representation than what the image-overflowing and mythologically centered religious texts were presenting.

The Indian religious texts contain an amalgam of theistic and nontheistic passages, and if we consider the particular ideas that Schopenhauer extracted from them for citation in *The World as Will and Representation*, it is evident that the nontheistic ideas drew his attention. These include (1) the conviction that the ordinary world of trees, rocks, roads, and people is illusory, or dreamlike (Schopenhauer had already absorbed this idea from his readings of Plato, Kant, Shakespeare, and Calderón), (2) the thought that at the world's foundation, there is an immediate distinction between its "inner" and "outer" natures (namely, "Atman" and "Brahman"), and (3) the proposition that by adopting an attitude of psychological detachment, as in yogic practice, we can achieve personal salvation. The import for him is this: although the external world is like a dream, and although that world has an inner nature that is more real than its dreamlike appearance, if we are careful not to become too consumed by either that external, dreamlike world, or the inner world that is its source, we can achieve a measure of liberation and enlightenment.

From 1814 to 1818, Schopenhauer lived in Dresden, where over a span of four years, he composed *The World as Will and Representation*. Schopenhauer had formulated almost all of his key ideas by the end of 1814, when he was 26 years old, and in the three years to follow, he developed and sharpened his assembly of basic insights. A leading question was whether Plato's Forms or Kant's supposedly unknowable "thing-in-itself" would reside at his theory's foundation. Schopenhauer eventually gravitated toward the latter, but in contrast to Kant, he rendered the "thing-in-itself" knowable and called it "Will."

Aiming to undermine the optimistic view that the world is fundamentally good and is slowly growing and getting better of its own accord, even as we engage in war, Schopenhauer described our daily world as a fundamentally bad scene. It is hopelessly frustrating, sinful, deceiving, disillusioning, empty, bankrupt, cheating, and agonizing. One of the most powerful words he uses is ὕπουλος [*hupoulos*], from ancient Greek, which conveys the image of lifting a bandage to reveal a festering wound, filled with sores and rotten flesh. This is what he sees when he looks beneath the world's often very beautiful surface.

At one of the dramatic points in *The World as Will and Representation* (§68), Schopenhauer relates the story of Ramon Lull (1232–1315) who, after lustfully and incessantly pursuing Ambrosia Eleonora de Castello de Genes, a married woman, finally found himself alone with her, expecting eagerly to fulfill his irrepressible desires. She removed her blouse, and contrary to Lull's expectations, did so to show that her breast had been terribly eaten away by cancer, and that he should desist in his advances. Lull, thoroughly horrified, subsequently made a conversion to penitence, and modelled his life on that of St. Francis of Assisi.

Such life-changing images and traumatic experiences contain the key feelings for understanding Schopenhauer's philosophy, for they illustrate how a person's once overwhelming, compelling, and promising desires can be immediately suspended, turned back upon themselves, and stilled. For Schopenhauer, the experience of being taken terribly aback from one's instinctual drives and having them quickly dissolve, is none other than an experience of enlightenment.

Schopenhauer uses powerful examples, but they extend to millions of less dramatic cases. Included here are all sorts of disappointing episodes where people initially project hopes, work hard toward a goal, construct a value system, and assign meaning to their lives, only to discover that when the goal is attained, it is less satisfying than how was imagined to be. Schopenhauer goes so far as to say that such disillusionment describes the human condition. He firmly believes that the ordinary game of life is not worth the candle.

Schopenhauer's writings subsequent to *The World as Will and Representation* rest upon his 1818 vision of the world. His next publication appears 18 years later, entitled *The Will in Nature* (1836), within which he tries to show how contemporary scientific views support his philosophy, and where he explores in addition to physiology, anatomy, linguistics, and astronomy, more uncommon subjects such as telepathy, magic, and Chinese philosophy. These various investigations are all directed toward showing that an impersonal Will underlies everything.

The sphere of ethics soon came to the forefront of Schopenhauer's attention and in 1839 he submitted an award-winning essay on the freedom of the will. A year later, he composed another essay on the foundations of morality, which he published together with the first essay the following year under the title, *The Two Fundamental Problems of Ethics* (1841). Despite his atheism, Schopenhauer never wavered from the idea that we should do no harm to others, and that the feeling of compassion is the essential moral feeling.

Ever since the publication of *The World as Will and Representation*, Schopenhauer conceived of a second volume to his main work, and he continually compiled notes for this over the next couple of decades. In 1844, he published that anticipated second volume, which is a set of essays that explicate and enhance the contents of the first. Many of the essays stand well on their own, and provide a good introduction to his philosophical outlook. Especially informative are ones that accompany Book Four of the first Volume, such as "On the Vanity and Suffering of Life" and "On the Doctrine of the Denial of the Will-to-Live."

Aside from a new, significantly expanded edition of his 1813 doctoral dissertation that was published in 1847, Schopenhauer's last major work was a two-volume set of essays entitled, *Parerga and Paralipomena* (1851)—a title that could be translated as "Accessories and Supplements." Like the second volume of *The World as Will and Representation*, these essays enrich his previously published ideas. In this final work, Schopenhauer writes more informally and accessibly to a larger audience, rendering it less of a surprise that after waiting a lifetime for some significant philosophical recognition, he finally saw his writings capture the interest of wider audiences through this publication. Today, his most-frequently reproduced essays are from this 1851 work, such as his essays on women and on suicide.

Schopenhauer's lifetime coincided with a number of political changes in Europe, but it is fair to say that his philosophy was written to stand timelessly above and independently of any particular social and political configurations. His opinion of

Napoleon is revealing in this regard. For Schopenhauer, Napoleon was an extraordinary man in his power to realize his desires. He was also a bad man with respect to the pain he caused, which, if we consider the depth of human and animal suffering involved in the 1812 invasion of Russia alone, stretches beyond comprehension. Yet Schopenhauer does not regard Napoleon as special. He sees him as common, and as nothing more than an example writ large of what everyone is naturally like. Some people might behave better than others, but on the whole, Schopenhauer perceives Napoleon as exemplifying the human norm.

To convey a sense of Schopenhauer's philosophy we can conclude this overture with an image from the second volume of *The World as Will and Representation*. Schopenhauer refers to the writings of Franz Wilhelm Junghuhn (1809–64) who, while in Java, encountered a field covered extensively with the skeletons of large turtles. All had been eaten alive by wild dogs after having come up from the sea to lay their eggs. Reflecting upon how this predatory scene had been repeated for centuries, and how horrible it is for the turtles, Schopenhauer asks himself what the point is. It is as if the turtles are born to be killed by the dogs. Similarly, as Voltaire once observed, it is as if flies are born to be killed by spiders. For Schopenhauer, there is no point, no upcoming heavenly society, and no glorious justification for the suffering that has been filling millennia. To him, the daily world remains fundamentally as it has always been, namely, a violent nightmare—one from which we should wake up, and secure some relief and escape. As we explore Schopenhauer's *The World as Will and Representation* in further detail, we will see why he is convinced that this is the case, and how salvation in a state of ineffable tranquillity is the final aim.

CHAPTER 2

OVERVIEW OF THEMES

SYNOPSIS OF THEMES IN THE PREFACES AND THE CRITIQUE OF KANT'S PHILOSOPHY

Schopenhauer asks us to read his book twice, since he constructs it as an organic unity expressive of a "single thought," with no first or last part, ideally conceived. This organically unified construction differs from that of preceding philosophies, the majority of which begin by setting down some supposedly certain foundation, and then proceed to build up, spin out, or grow further philosophical contents from that original basis in a quasi-mechanical manner. With his emphasis upon organic unity, Schopenhauer hopes to present a philosophy that is more animated than his predecessors.

Despite the object-oriented, scientific quality that Kant's philosophy displays, Schopenhauer is inspired by Kant, and is particularly captivated by his doctrines of space and time. For Kant, space and time are not mind-independent realities, but are interpretive features of the human mind. Since we always interpret as we perceive, and consequently invoke the forms of space and time to inform our perception, the world of daily experience that we construct does not represent how things really are. It represents only how reality appears to us through our human, spatio-temporal lens. For this reason, Schopenhauer maintains that ordinary life is illusory, like a dream. He derives this idea from Kant, who referred to the daily world as a world of mere appearances.

To appreciate the leading thought behind Kant's and Schopenhauer's views, we can imagine any situation where we are speaking with another person. From our standpoint external to the person, we can observe the person's bodily movements, hear the person's voice, and in principle, could scientifically explore every atom of the person's body. No matter how far we might explore on this external level, however, we would never come into direct contact with the person's consciousness which, presumably like our own, is at the center of the person's experience, and which is itself experienced by the person as not being an object at all.

From our external standpoint, we only have the person's appearances to apprehend and in this sense, the person's consciousness remains forever invisible to us. Indeed, our respective consciousnesses are all invisible to one another. This is the same kind of inaccessibility Kant and Schopenhauer apprehend when we try to reveal the inner nature of things through scientific observation. They believe that the effort is fruitless, which leaves us to conclude that we have only appearances with which to deal immediately, at least when we look outward toward objects other than ourselves.

Since Kant was writing in the late 1700s, he was still wedded to the scientific worldview that interprets the world exclusively in terms of material objects that are causally related to each other. This is the ordinary world conceived as a large mechanism, like a clock, and it is why Kant's philosophy is filled with phrasings that refer to "objects" and "causes." At one crucial point, Kant applies these concepts to metaphysical reality, saying that an absolute object—the thing-in-itself—causes our perceptions, or apprehensions of appearances.

Schopenhauer reminds us that according to Kant, although the concepts of "object" and "cause" can be used in a non-committal, speculative way, they cannot be used legitimately to apply knowingly to the thing-in-itself. This indicates for Schopenhauer, if we are to refer to such a condition in a substantial way, that we should not use the terms "object" or "cause." For him, the thing-in-itself is not an object, nor does it cause anything to happen. We consequently need an alternative vocabulary to describe the relationship between the thing-in-itself and our experience. Schopenhauer later provides one by introducing the terms "objectification" and "manifestation" in place of "causality," and says that the fundamental spirit within us—Will—fashions through us, the world we experience.

SYNOPSIS OF THEMES IN BOOK I, §§1–16

Book I begins *WWR* proper, and Schopenhauer asserts immediately that "the world is my representation." By this, he means that the world before us, considered objectively as a "representation" or "object," is only the set of our immediate perceptions in conjunction with our sea of memories. These perceptions and memories are reflections of ourselves, for they are structured according to the way we must experience things, namely, in space, time, and as objects in causal relationships to each other. Our sensations are subjective, our modes of structuring those sensations are subjective, and whatever the source of our sensations happens to be, it cannot be a mind-independent object, as he believes his critique of Kant's philosophy has shown.

Given this, Schopenhauer states that the only objects of which we are aware are our representations, or mental images, and there is nothing beyond them in terms of representations. Specifically, there are no free-floating, mind-independent mental images. To assert otherwise would be contradictory, since every mental image must be an image in some mind or other. The world is "representation," and every representation presupposes a subject that has it in mind.

The immediately known representations constitute perceptual experience, and for Schopenhauer, everything is built up from these perceptions. This basis he calls "intuitive" or "perceptual" knowledge. It is distinguished from the set of abstract concepts that we construct out of our perceptual experience, all of which are merely summations and derivations of that experience. "Perception" has philosophical and experiential priority over "conception" on Schopenhauer's view. In this respect, Schopenhauer deviates from his ideal of organic unity, and asserts a more foundation-oriented style of philosophizing.

The bulk of Book I aims to show how perception precedes conception in some important ways. Contrary to traditional views, but consistent with Kant, Schopenhauer argues that mathematics and geometry are not based on abstract definitions and logical implication, but are grounded upon on the structures of space and time. He adds that the purely conceptual part of Kant's philosophy—Kant's theory of the understanding—is mostly a construction of empty and derivative abstract concepts, and that what is worth retaining is only the aspect that is intimately and importantly linked with perception, namely, the concept of causality.

Schopenhauer argues further that Kant's ethics—yet another area within Kant's philosophy that is based on pure conception—misrepresents the nature of ethical awareness. Stoic ethics as well—an ethics based on reason, and a cousin to Kant's ethical theory—is said to offer the wrong path to enlightened living. Schopenhauer accepts many Stoic insights and conclusions, but he rejects the rationalistic means that the Stoics use to attain their moral goals.

At the end of Book I, we realize that Schopenhauer has been developing the idea that science—the objective view of things—cannot provide us with metaphysical knowledge. Science rests on the principle of sufficient reason, which is to say that it is based on relationships of necessity that are exclusively human-relative, and hence as far as we can know, not in the fabric of things in themselves. Since science has this metaphysically unpromising grounding, Schopenhauer indicates that we must penetrate beyond the objective surface of things that the world as representation offers, to arrive at the metaphysical truth and awareness that we seek. This entails looking inward for philosophical truths, rather than outward.

SYNOPSIS OF THEMES IN BOOK II, §§17–29

Book II begins by reiterating that mathematics, geometry, the derivation of abstract ideas from experience, along with all philosophy that grounds itself upon the concept of causality, are all unable to provide insight into the inner nature of things. These disciplines stick to the surface and never penetrate beyond that surface. To have a metaphysical awareness, we need to approach things along a different route.

Looking for a way to apprehend the inner reality of the things in the world, Schopenhauer realizes that there is one thing among the world's many things, namely, his own physical body, which gives him direct contact with that thing's inner reality. When feeling the nature of his own inner reality at its most original level, he labels it "Will," to capture the sense of the raw, driving urge that he feels that he is. Convinced that he has apprehended the inner nature of one of the representations within his perceptual field—and this apprehension is crucial to his philosophy—he reasons that all of the other representations must have the same kind of inner reality. Otherwise, his perceptual field would be riddled with absurdities.

Recalling his account of the principle of sufficient reason where he argues that all forms of multiplicity stem from that principle, and adding that the principle of sufficient reason determines not how things really are, but only how they appear, Schopenhauer maintains that the inner reality of the entire perceptual field is "one" and that Will is the sole, uniform reality. Will manifests itself as the field of perceptual representations. It does not "cause" that field. It "is" that field of perceptual representations, just as ice cubes and steam are "water" in the sense of being H_2O through and through.

Will expresses itself in a set of timeless acts, or Platonic Ideas, each of which is the respective intelligible character of the individuals that we experience in time and space. The hierarchy of Platonic Ideas ranges from the essences of inorganic beings, to those of plants, animals, and humans, with accordingly harmonious and disharmonious relationships among the Ideas. The instantiations of the Ideas, such as individual cats and birds, spiders and flies, good and evil, reflect these harmonies and disharmonies, and in the case of disharmonious Ideas, the instantiations battle forever within the spatio-temporal world. These combating individuals do not matter in the wider scheme of things, since the tensions and balances between the timeless Ideas are governing the world of appearances. The dreamlike, spatio-temporal world is consequently one of constantly competing, constantly struggling individuals, that rise up, fall down, recycle, and eternally recur in an arena filled with violence and suffering. The arena is essentially pointless. It makes no sense to ask what "Will" is aiming for. It has no aim.

Given the meaninglessness of the world as representation, Schopenhauer sets out to find some temporary relief and salvation from the world's ups and downs, births and deaths, and desires and disappointments. This leads us into Book III, where he introduces aesthetic awareness as a mode of transcendence and inner tranquillity.

In sum, Books I and II describe the human situation as a prison of incessant desire; Books III and IV describe various means of liberation from this spatio-temporal detention center and world of suffering. In this respect, the first half of *WWR* is about naturally given constraints; the second is about the quest for freedom.

SYNOPSIS OF THEMES IN BOOK III, §§30–52

The distinction between subject and object can occur at either the individual level or the universal level. At the individual level, we find ourselves in the ordinary world of spatio-temporal objects and desire. At the universal level, we realize ourselves as relatively time-free, desire-free subjects who are correspondingly aware of timeless objects, the Platonic Ideas. The apprehension of a Platonic Idea is also the apprehension of beauty, for according to Schopenhauer, beauty is the immediate presentation of an object's perfect and timeless form. The experience of beauty valuably lifts us temporarily from the ordinary world of desires and transient satisfactions, and situates us in a realm of tranquillity where time seems to stand still.

Most people lack a strong and consistent ability to apprehend the Platonic Ideas that shine through ordinary things, but artistic geniuses, who naturally possess this ability, can replicate the contents of their visions of the Ideas in works of art, and thereby help others attain a measure of peace through the work of art's presentation. In this respect, artistic geniuses perform a suffering-alleviating service to humanity.

The subject-matter of works of art can range over the entire hierarchy of Platonic Ideas, and certain forms of art are more suited to certain levels in the hierarchy than others. Architecture best expresses the lower Ideas of inorganic nature. The other arts expressive of Platonic Ideas—sculpture, painting, and poetry—can include as their subjects a wide array of Ideas, but as we move up the hierarchy, poetic (or literary) art emerges as the highest, most appropriate way to convey the many-sided Idea of humanity. Within the field of poetic art itself, tragedy resides at the summit, since it artistically presents the inherent suffering of human existence most clearly.

The art of music transports us more thoroughly into the realm of human subjectivity, for it expresses the formal essences of human emotional life. Sadness itself, happiness itself, gaiety itself, are all expressed through music, and in this sense, Schopenhauer refers to music as the direct copy of Will, rather than as a presentation of Platonic Ideas, and as different in kind from the other arts.

Music presents emotional life in a painless but also formal and abstracted way, far removed from the actual human experiences themselves. It offers peace for this reason, but it also gives us a less than realistic apprehension of humanity's terrible sufferings. To grasp humanity's consciousness in a truer, realistic, and more concrete way, it is necessary to move beyond the merely aesthetic appreciation of human emotion that music offers. We need to engage empathetically with other people and try to feel exactly what they feel. This is the path to moral awareness and eventually to asceticism, which Schopenhauer describes in Book IV.

SYNOPSIS OF THEMES IN BOOK IV, §§53–71

Book IV brings Schopenhauer's "single thought" of which his philosophy is the expression, into the field of social activity, which he describes loosely as the ethical world. Assuming that the fundamental human condition is thoroughly selfish, confrontational, and steeped in metaphysical ignorance, Schopenhauer describes increasingly more enlightened forms of awareness that emerge as the common identity of everyone and everything in Will becomes more obvious.

Starting with the selfish condition, Schopenhauer defines the activity of interfering with others' selfish desires as "wrong," and the noninterference with others as "right." More precisely, "wrong" is what is not permissible, and "right" is what is permissible. The "bad" person does wrong whenever the opportunity presents itself, and the "just" person, although selfish, tries decently not to interfere with the activities of other selfish individuals.

The "noble" person lives on higher plane of metaphysical awareness, realizing that others are of essentially the same substance as himself or herself, compassionately feeling the pain of others as if it were his or her own. The noble person does not harm other people, and goes to great lengths to avoid causing suffering to any living being.

The saintly person has the same kind of compassionate awareness, but across a wider scope and at a higher intensity, identifying with all of the world's suffering. At this level, the saint appreciates that the energy that constitutes himself or herself, namely Will, constitutes the world, and that Will is the being that produces all suffering and death. This generates a sense of self-repulsion and disgust at the nature of the universe, now apprehended as an inherently poisonous energy that flows through everything. In reaction to this morally upsetting condition, present both inside and out, the saint acts contrary to Will's natural tendencies as they are manifested in individuals. For instance, the saint acts nonsexually when sexual feelings emerge, nonmaterialistically when acquisitive tendencies show themselves, nonviolently, when aggressive feelings are present, and so on.

The final state of complete denial of the will-to-live compares to having conquered an all-permeating addiction. It is a burden-free, almost mystical, condition, fully liberated from the world of alluring and frustrating desire. It is a state of suspension and detachment where the world appears devoid of illusory attraction, much as one might perceive a once-blazing costume, thrown onto the floor after the party has ended. It is a condition of supreme liberation, which Schopenhauer associates in the final lines of *The World as Will and Representation* with the Buddhist perfection of wisdom.

CHAPTER 3

READING THE TEXT

SECTION 1. SCHOPENHAUER'S PREFACES TO *WWR*, HIS CRITIQUE OF THE KANTIAN PHILOSOPHY, AND *THE FOURFOLD ROOT OF THE PRINCIPLE OF SUFFICIENT REASON*

THE PREFACES TO *WWR*

Schopenhauer included a preface to each of the three editions of *WWR* and each reveals an important feature of the text and its reception. With noticeable specificity, the first edition preface of 1818 outlines the philosophical background we should have before attempting to read the book; the second edition preface of 1844 reveals Schopenhauer's embittered feelings of neglect at age 56, after having waited a quarter of a century to see *WWR* have a social impact; the third edition preface of September 1859 reveals Schopenhauer's satisfaction after having finally enjoyed a few years of recognition for his philosophical contributions, writing then at the age of 71, along with his hopes for future recognition. Schopenhauer's life came to a close exactly a year later, in September 1860.

For our immediate purposes, the first preface is the most valuable, since it contains Schopenhauer's idea of the preparation that his readers require for understanding *WWR*, which we will follow. His initial and emphatic advice is to "read the book twice," for it constitutes "a single thought," organically structured, where the end presupposes the beginning and the beginning presupposes the end. As he conceives of his work, any given part presupposes all the other parts for its adequate comprehension.

Second, Schopenhauer reminds us in 1818 that his 1813 doctoral dissertation, *The Fourfold Root of the Principle of Sufficient Reason*, is the proper introduction to *WWR*, and he believes that if his readers do not first absorb the contents of the dissertation, his book cannot be well understood. Third, he adds that a familiarity with Kant's critical philosophy is necessary, since he conceives of *WWR* as a more coherent expression and development of Kant's main insights. Such are, then, the chief desiderata: we should understand the main tenets of Kant's philosophy, Schopenhauer's doctoral dissertation, and then read *WWR* twice.

If the situation were ideal, Schopenhauer adds that his readers would be well-prepared to grasp his message, if there were a further acquaintance with Plato's philosophy, and best of all prepared if they had read the *Vedas* and *Upanishads*. We will concentrate on the initial three desiderata in this chapter, and introduce Plato and the ancient Indian texts as they arise later in Schopenhauer's exposition.

The World as Will and Representation as "a single thought"

When examining Schopenhauer's dissertation and manuscript notes for *WWR*, it is a small, but gratifying, surprise to see that he appears indeed to have envisioned the book "all at once" when he was 25–26 years old, during the years 1813–14. *WWR* divides into four parts that respectively address the theory of knowledge, metaphysics, aesthetics, and ethics, and when one surveys his doctoral dissertation of 1813 and his notebook entries from 1814, it becomes evident that most of *WWR*'s key ideas were formulated before the end of 1814. Schopenhauer tells us in the preface to *WWR* that the book represents a "single thought," and there is good reason to take him at his word.

This presence of a tightly woven interdependency among his philosophy's aspects contrasts with what Schopenhauer refers to subordinatingly as a more simple-minded way to philosophize, namely in terms of building a "system" of philosophy. Using the term "system" in a nonstandard sense, he refers to this philosophical style as one where an assumedly self-evident foundational basis is initially set, from which all of the philosophy's other aspects are then developed either as logical or psychological extensions. The so-called systematic structure is thus asymmetrical: the extensions depend upon the foundation, but the foundation does not depend on the extensions.

These philosophical foundations could, for instance, be a set of definitions or axioms, from which other propositions are logically implied, as we find in rationalist philosophy. Baruch Spinoza's *Ethics* (1677) is exemplary, as it starts with self-evident definitions that provide the elements of axiomatic expressions, and continues with a complicated sequence of logically implied propositions, proofs, and corollaries that build upon one another, like a treatise on geometry.

Alternatively, the foundation could be a set of elementary sensory experiences—for example, red, green, blue, hard, soft, loud, quiet, rough, smooth, etc.—from which perceptions of ordinary objects are then psychologically constructed. John Locke's empiricism exemplifies this second approach. The foundation could also be a single concept from which all other concepts, and eventually the world itself, sprouts. Hegel's system of philosophy is the prime example, where its seeds are in abstract logic and its elemental concept of "being." These logical seeds develop into the presence of solid inanimate nature, and from within that inanimate nature, the gradual realization and materialization of logical forms generates life and human society.

Schopenhauer had Spinoza, Locke, Fichte, and Schelling (the latter two in the place of Hegel, since Hegel's system in his *Encyclopedia* was constructed contemporaneously with Schopenhauer's, around 1817) in mind as examples of philosophers with whom he wanted to oppose his own style of holistic philosophizing. Insofar as these antecedent philosophers were all seeking steady foundations, they theorized within the tradition inspired by Descartes, who sought in his *Meditations on First Philosophy* (1641) an indubitable foundation upon which to ground his own philosophy, which, as is well-known, he found in the act of immediate self-awareness, or *cogito* ("I think").

Unlike philosophers who conceive of philosophizing as akin to spinning a web, building a house, or growing a plant from a seed, Schopenhauer conceives of philosophical activity as a more immediately visionary enterprise, where all of the vision's components present themselves as a single, integrated insight, like a ready-formed organism. This is why he places the equivalent of a musical *da capo* at the end of *WWR*, signalling that we should "play it again, from the beginning" to comprehend the work fully.

"Organic unity" as a nineteenth-century inspirational idea

When Schopenhauer was writing in the second decade of the nineteenth century, the seventeenth- and eighteenth-century mechanistic view of the world was in the process of being replaced by a more lively model. The image of the world as a clockwork, running predictably, exactly, and inevitably according to mathematically defined natural laws, had been of tremendous advantage in the development of physics, as is evident in the work of Galileo and Newton. It was also crucial in the realm of technical discovery, as displayed in the development during this period of the telescope (1608), slide rule (c. 1620), barometer (1643), air pump (1650), pendulum clock (1656), steam engine (1698), and sextant (1731), among other inventions.

This image of the clockwork soon extended to include the workings of the human body, and this led to positive advances in medicine and biology. The image also made its way into the workplace as well, introducing a robotic conception of workers as parts of a social machine to be used and replaced when inefficiently operating. As a growing sense of dehumanization began to take hold, the attractiveness of the mechanistic model began to fade. Philosophical issues concerning human freedom also became salient—Kant himself had already begun to address them in the 1780s and 1790s—for it was increasingly difficult to imagine how humans could be free, if every physical movement is a predictable part of a seamless natural mechanism.

Adding to such concerns, it was also widely felt that religious inspiration was waning and that the social participation at local houses of worship was becoming mechanical, with the majority of people losing sight of genuine spiritual values. Writing in 1816, Schopenhauer was perceiving around him that religion had "almost entirely died out."[1]

Side-by-side with the deadening effects that the mechanistic interpretation of the world was engendering, the nineteenth-century atmosphere within which Schopenhauer was writing, harbored feelings of disunity and disintegration with respect to political, philosophic, social, and personal spheres. These issued in a search for unity along a number of dimensions.

Despite the political dominance of Prussia and Bavaria, hundreds of principalities still divided the German-speaking world into a chaotic patchwork when Schopenhauer was writing

WWR. Kant's influential philosophy additionally had inscribed difficult-to-bridge divisions between appearance and reality, body and soul, sensation and conception, science and morality, knowledge and faith, and determinism and freedom. This stimulated efforts to reintegrate these divisions by means of a more unified and life-oriented vision of the world.

Such assorted pressures produced a change in the main concepts and models employed in philosophizing, and with the passage from the eighteenth century to the nineteenth century, mechanistic thinking slowly became unseated by organically focused, unity-oriented imagery and theorizing. Hegel's system of philosophy, mentioned above, is an illustrative case, for it retains the earlier foundationalist style of seeking a firm grounding, from which issue further developments (in his case, dialectically), but adds an organically unifying dimension to this extension by importing as its main inspiration and model, the central image of a plant that grows from a seed.

At the start of the nineteenth century, the concept of "life" thus appears more saliently in philosophical theories, and the concept of "organic unity" presents itself as one of the initial expressions of the reaction against mechanistic thinking. These two notions—"life" and "organic unity"—variously interpreted, establish the tone of much nineteenth-century philosophy. The organic structure of Schopenhauer's *WWR*, and his recommendation that we read the book twice is an artifact of this historical atmosphere.

Nineteenth-century revivifying strategies

We can identify two ways in which theorists at the beginning of the nineteenth century attempted to inject some life into their theorizing and visions of the world. Both involve the search for a healthier or authentically spiritual condition, given the prevailing religious and cultural sentiments. The first was to invoke the spirit of ancient Greece, since it was then common to believe that the ancient Greeks had been the healthiest, most integrated, and most exemplary of human cultures. The second was to search for the originally inspiring essence of Christianity, which had apparently become lost. This search often amounted to formulating what it would be like to have a consciousness akin to what Jesus himself experienced, since this would embody a truly Christian mentality. We will see some of this Christianity in Schopenhauer.

Despite his famous interest in Hinduism and Buddhism, Schopenhauer can be understood as attempting to inform his philosophy with the true message of Christianity—a message that he believes recommends asceticism as the path to salvation—with the hope that others will absorb that Christian message to reduce their own suffering, along with the suffering in the world. It helps here to note a double-aspectedness in the notion of "life" that nineteenth-century theorists were using in their philosophies, where life sometimes assumes a friendly, organic-unity-focused, well-integrated, and balanced countenance, and at other times, an unfriendly, violent, and vicious one. Schopenhauer initially emphasizes organic unity, but in another segment of his philosophy, his emphasis upon life's more violent aspects is more pronounced. As we will see, the latter is relevant to how he can be interpreted as a fundamentally Christian philosopher who regards the daily world as an illusion and penitentiary, and who coincidentally notices the same ideas inspirationally in Hinduism and Buddhism.

In contrast, despite his characterization of world history as a "slaughter bench," Hegel represents philosophers who conceive of life in a positive way, all things considered, as involving balance, organic unity, development, fluidity, and rationality. To be healthy, or to exemplify life well, one would integrate body and soul, remain in psychological equilibrium, develop one's potentials, organize one's life according to a rational plan, and perhaps spice one's overall outlook with some temperate wisdom. Here, "life" has a friendly and promising presentation.

As mentioned, life's vicious, competitive, hurtful, aggressive, expansive, appropriative, disillusioning, and essentially amoral dimensions of experience do not escape Schopenhauer's notice. In fact, these aspects of life constitute a hard truth for him, against which his philosophy reacts. One cannot live without killing other living things and consuming them for nourishment, and if one does not learn how to be aggressive, then one may easily become food for some other being or person. This is an instinctual, nonrationally governed conception of life that for Schopenhauer, underlies the world of selfish desire.

23

When life is interpreted in this way, one is led to ask with greater puzzlement, what its value is. On the face of things, one eats and drinks simply to become hungry and thirsty once again, and one begets beings like oneself, so that they will do the same once more, pointlessly. In the absence of a positive conception of life, where growth and development provide hope, this more violent conception brings one face-to-face with nihilism. Schopenhauer accordingly states that life is a sad and senseless joke, but he resists concluding that the human condition is hopeless. To resolve this tension, he turns to the relatively time-free experiences of beauty and the minimization of desire, as we will see in Books III and IV of *WWR*.

SCHOPENHAUER'S DOCTORAL DISSERTATION: *THE FOURFOLD ROOT OF THE PRINCIPLE OF SUFFICIENT REASON*

The principle of sufficient reason expresses the natural idea that the world is not absurd, and that for any given fact or true proposition, there is a reason why that fact or proposition is such. It is in our human nature to ask "why?" without restriction. The principle of sufficient reason states that for any condition, whether it happens to be that Arthur Schopenhauer was born on February 22, 1788, that the earth has one moon, or that the perceivable universe is in space and time, there is always some explanation. These reasons or explanations might presently be unknown, and might never be known, but the principle states that such reasons and explanations exist. For any field of inquiry where the principle of sufficient reason is assumed to apply, it follows that that field of inquiry is believed to be thoroughly understandable in principle. Once we apply the principle of sufficient reason to the field of possible human experience, we assume that human life contains no genuine absurdities. Once we apply it to being as a whole, we assume that the rational is the real and that the real is the rational.

Using the principle of sufficient reason, one can argue that the earth could not have been moving through space when it was created, for there is no reason why it would be moving in one direction rather than another, since all directions in space are equally valued. One can argue that since all points in time are the same in quality, the universe could not have been created at any particular point in time, for there is no reason to create the universe at any one point as opposed to another. One can argue that no two individuals are exactly alike, since there would be no reason why one individual would be in one place, and the other in another place. One can argue furthermore that space is not an objective reality, for although it appears to contain incongruent counterparts such as right and left hands, there is no reason why God would have formed space in a predominantly right-handed or left-handed direction, and hence, no reason why there should be such asymmetries in reality. The governing idea in these examples is that if some proposition can have no possible reasons in its support, then the proposition cannot be true.

On the constructive side, Schopenhauer observes that whenever there is something to explain, several conditions must obtain. First, there must be a subject or someone who is seeking an explanation. Second, there must be something that that person wants to explain. Third, if the explanation is to be legitimate, then the explanation cannot be arbitrary or merely tentative, but must be necessary. These thoughts are at the very root of the principle of sufficient reason, and they lead Schopenhauer to maintain that at the most fundamental level of explanation, at the principle's root, we must presuppose: (1) the subject-object distinction, which when present, entails the appearance always of both a subject and an object in relation to each other, and (2) links between the components of the explanation that are necessary, for if the linkages are not necessary, then there is no true explanation. If there is no subject who seeks an explanation, then there can be no object of awareness to be explained. When there are subjects who are aware of objects, then these objects of awareness are "representations" (*Vorstellungen*), or mental images. Conversely, if there is an object, or representation, then there must be a subject in which that representation appears.

Expanding upon this "root" of the principle of sufficient reason, Schopenhauer identifies four different *kinds* of necessary connection that can appear in explanations. Through this itemization, he intends to exhaust all the varieties of necessary connection with the hope of establishing the foundation of a general theory of explanation. He believes that this foundation had not yet been well defined, for the preceding history of philosophy always contained the uncritical assumption that "reason" is a single concept, equally applicable in all kinds of circumstances. Schopenhauer maintains, though, that the concept of "reason" is like the concept of "triangle": if there is a triangle, it exclusively must be equilateral, isosceles, or scalene. We must analogously specify the *kind* of reason we are employing when we apply our rationality, that is, when we look for explanations.

Schopenhauer accordingly identifies four kinds of reason and four kinds of corresponding objects that can operate within explanations, again exclusively. We can be interested in (1) explaining the conditions of physical things, for which *causal* explanation is appropriate, (2) explaining relationships between concepts, for which *logical* explanation is appropriate, (3) explaining relationships between numbers, formulae, or geometrical figures, for which *mathematical/geometrical* explanation is appropriate, or (4) explaining motivations, inner drives, or the presence of subjective states of mind, for which motive-referring, *psychological* explanation is appropriate.

One of Schopenhauer's key tenets is that once we choose the kind of object to be explained, we must hold fast to the kind of explanation that is appropriate to that kind of object, and resist introducing styles of reasoning that are appropriate to some other kind of object. For example, it would not make sense on his view to explain some physical object's presence and/or condition, by referring to pure definitions and the process of logical implication. Here, the relevant kind of necessary connection is not logical implication, but causal connection between physical objects or events. Similarly, one would not genuinely explain why a person felt that he or she should pay a debt and acted accordingly to pay the debt, by referring to neurological firings in the person's brain that correlated with the action. The first example involves confusing causal with logical explanation; the second example involves confusing causal explanation with psychological explanation.

The illegitimacy of such criss-crossings and interminglings of different kinds of reason-giving compares to a person who squeezes cranberries or strawberries and expects grape juice to emerge. Schopenhauer discerns that many philosophers have nonetheless displayed such confusions in explanation, often in the foundational propositions in their philosophies. As far as Schopenhauer can see, these illegitimate foundations usually involve the acceptance of the ontological argument for God's existence, which he regards as based on exactly the kind of confusion he is urging his readers to guard against. The ontological argument starts with mere conceptual definitions (viz., "God is a being than which no greater can be conceived") and concludes dramatically by positing an existent being (viz., "God exists"). According to Schopenhauer, this confuses logical explanation with causal explanation.

The phrase "principle of sufficient reason" appears throughout *WWR*. Schopenhauer is emphatic about restricting the scope of the principle, and argues that it can be used to refer to the entire set of necessary connections for human experience that Kant describes. For Kant, these are space, time, and twelve pure concepts of the understanding. For Schopenhauer, there are space, time, and the single concept of the understanding that Schopenhauer continues to recognize, namely, the concept of causality. In either inventory, these forms are ascribed to the human mind exclusively, and they define our capacity to know things scientifically. They are not features of the world as it is in itself, but are only features of our human way of knowing. Schopenhauer consequently refers to the principle of sufficient reason as one that generates for us the illusory world of space, time, and objects that interact with each other in a thorough going causal mechanism.

SCHOPENHAUER'S CRITICISM OF KANT'S THEORY OF KNOWLEDGE

Schopenhauer includes an appendix to *WWR* entitled, "Criticism of the Kantian Philosophy," which he recommends as a preliminary way to familiarize ourselves with the theoretical motives underlying his philosophy that stem from Kant. Schopenhauer sympathizes with Kant's outlook, but he discerns some errors in Kant's position that when corrected, imply the kind of metaphysics that Schopenhauer offers in Kant's place. The errors mainly concern Kant's understanding and characterization of the kind of metaphysical entity that supposedly causes our sensations, which he refers to as the "thing-in-itself." For Kant, this is an absolute, mind-independent reality that is what it is, whether or not we happen to be on the scene, as one might imagine the way God exists. Kant maintains that this thing-in-itself is unknowable as it is "in itself": at best, and forever our human fate, we can know only how this reality appears to us, and never how it truly is.

According to Kant, metaphysical knowledge is impossible, for we are beings that inevitably introduce our human nature into the situation whenever we know something. We are rational—and for Kant this signifies logical—beings and we thereby order our given sensations in rational sequences. We also order them in terms of space and time, which are geometrically and mathematically describable. This logic, space, and time are inherent in us as human beings, and we have no choice but to experience the world in their terms. How the world might be in itself is an independent matter, and since as finite human beings, we cannot experience the world otherwise than according to our logically ordered, spatio-temporal forms, we must rest content with the particular appearance of the world that they construct. To a nonhuman being, mind-independent reality will appear differently, if that being's experience is not informed by space, time, and logical forms.

Kant recognizes from the history of logic, twelve basic logical forms and accordingly, twelve corresponding concepts that we use to construct our experience. For Schopenhauer, the most important of these logical forms is the conditional form, "*If A, then B*," and as noted in the previous section, the concept of causality that is coordinated with it. Schopenhauer speaks consequently of "space, time and causality" as the primary forms through which we organize our experience. He is convinced that animals also experience the world in terms of these same three forms, and that they, too, have an "understanding" in this rudimentary sense. Crucial for both Kant and Schopenhauer is the idea that space, time, and causality do not tell us how things are in themselves, but only how mind-independent reality appears. Our application of the forms of space, time, and causality to our given sensations does nonetheless produce the shared world of human experience, although that world remains only an appearance of a higher, unknowable reality.

At one juncture, Schopenhauer notes how Kant is inconsistent when he states that the thing-in-itself "causes" our sensations,
virtually in the strict, scientific sense that compares to how a hot
flame causes water to boil. It is natural to speak in this way, since
we experience objects (e.g., hot plates or ice cubes) that cause
sensations in everyday contexts, and it is easy to extrapolate into
the larger context to refer to some mind-independent object that
causes our sensations as a whole in just the same way. This is
exactly what Kant does at one point, when he states that just as
a rainbow is an appearance produced by tiny particles of rain,
the tiny particles of rain themselves, and by extension, all other
physical objects, are appearances caused by the thing- in-itself.[2]

The inconsistency resides in Kant's own admission that we
cannot say knowingly that the thing-in-itself causes anything,
since the relationship of causality yields knowledge, only when it
holds between items that are situated in space and time. Since
the thing-in-itself is in neither time nor space, the relationship
of causality cannot apply knowingly to it. This precludes the
following argument: we experience sensations, and since there
must be some cause of those sensations—and hence, this cause
cannot itself be a sensation—then there must be some thing-
in-itself that is their cause and which is not in space and time. If
we reject this argument, following Schopenhauer, the resulting
position becomes strange, for we then have the mystery of where
our sensations collectively come from, if we cannot say that they
are "caused" by anything. Schopenhauer's philosophy aims to
answer this question and meet this challenge.

In parallel with the above reasoning, Schopenhauer argues
that Kant cannot legitimately refer to the thing-in-itself as an
"object," since the notion of an object is itself exclusively an
expression of the principle of sufficient reason, as one pole of
the "subject-object" distinction that is present in all knowledge
and that is at the principle of sufficient reason's root. Just as
with respect to knowledge, the concept of *causality* applies to
appearances only, the concept of an *object*, with respect to
knowledge, applies to appearances only. It is as problematic
to refer to the thing-in-itself as an object, as it is to say that it
causes anything.

This all implies that if one acknowledges a being called the
"thing-in-itself," then this being will not be an object and it will

not bear causal relations to anything. One of the outcomes of Schopenhauer's critique of Kant is to eliminate the words "cause" and "object" from references to and discussions about the thing-in-itself. Whatever the thing-in-itself is—and Schopenhauer acknowledges that there is a thing-in-itself—it is not a "thing" of any kind, contrary to how Kant conceptualized it.

Consider the perception of a table. When we apprehend it as the appearance of some non-perceivable reality, it is easy to imagine this latter as the table "in itself" or as the "transcendental table," conceived of as the imperceptible object that causes the perceived table to appear. This is the kind of reasoning that Schopenhauer emphatically rejects. Following his understanding of the principle of sufficient reason, he holds that the so-called transcendental object (in this case, it would be the transcendental table) is only an abstract concept that we construct from our perception of the table. The concept depends on the perceived table, not the other way around.

According to Schopenhauer, the perception of the actual table comes experientially and philosophically first, and in reference to this perception, a process of abstraction constructs the thought of the table "in itself" or of the "transcendental table." The latter is only an abstraction, though, and so it would be thinking in reverse to maintain that the abstraction causes our table-like perceptions, as when it is said that the transcendental table causes our perception of the spatio-temporal table.

Schopenhauer describes this confusion and reversal as due to conflating the sensory apprehension of objects, or what he calls "intuitive perception" or "intuitive knowledge" with the construction of abstract concepts on the basis of those intuitive perceptions. Following the British empiricists in this context, Schopenhauer maintains that all abstract concepts derive from intuitive perceptions. If so, then it is absurd to refer to an abstract concept as the cause of the very perceptions from which an abstraction was made to create that concept. This compares to looking at a full moon, abstracting the concept of a circle from the image, and then maintaining that the concept of the circle caused the moon to exist. For this reason, Schopenhauer refers repeatedly to Kant's "terrible" confusion between intuitive knowledge and abstract knowledge.

This supposed confusion between intuitive knowledge and abstract knowledge on Kant's part, leads Schopenhauer to reject the bulk of Kant's account of the human understanding. For Kant, our understanding is composed of twelve pure concepts that are expressive of twelve elementary forms of logical judgment, all of which derive from Aristotle's conception of logic. The stability and reliability of Aristotelian logic from the days of Aristotle up until Kant's own time convinced Kant of its legitimacy and expressiveness of our rational nature as human beings.

Schopenhauer maintains that with the exception of the concept of causality, the remaining eleven categories are abstract concepts that are not necessary for perceptual knowledge. He believes that most of the concepts are arrived at through abstraction from experience. Whether or not this is true, part of Schopenhauer's motivation for rejecting Kant's categories is his observation that animals do not seem to have these concepts (viz., unity, plurality, totality, reality, negation, limitation, substance, reciprocity, possibility, actuality, necessity) and yet they have no difficulties perceiving tables, chairs, trees, food, other animals, and the like. So Schopenhauer concludes that the only category of the understanding that should be retained is the concept of causality, which we share with the animals. This yields space, time, and causality as the *a priori* forms of experience. We will see that Schopenhauer sometimes refers to space and time by themselves as the "principle of individuation" (the *principium individuationis*) when the context is appropriate:

> We know that *plurality* in general is necessarily conditioned by time and space, and only in these is conceivable, and in this respect we call them the *principium individuationis*. (§24)

STUDY QUESTIONS

1. Does Schopenhauer regard himself as having developed a "system" of philosophy? Why or why not?
2. What is the principle of sufficient reason?
3. What is the "root" of the principle of sufficient reason?
4. What is the "fourfold" root of the principle of sufficient reason, and why would Schopenhauer consequently reject

any philosophy that is based on the ontological argument for God's existence?

5. Why does Schopenhauer believe that the words "cause" and "object" do not apply legitimately to metaphysical reality (i.e., the "thing-in-itself") as it is in itself?

SECTION 2. BOOK I, PERCEPTUAL VS. ABSTRACT REPRESENTATIONS, §§1–16

The long subtitle of Book I reads: "The representation considered under the conditions of the principle of sufficient reason: the object of experience and science." Schopenhauer refers here to the world that we ordinarily apprehend—the world of tables, chairs, rocks, stars, trees, other people, etc.—as it stands before us in space and time, and as it is filled with objects that are causally related to each other. This world is an immense set of representations. As such, Schopenhauer attends in Book I to how the world appears to us as an objective, mechanically operating, scientifically understandable entity, constituted by measurable items, as we encounter it observationally in daily experience. This is the world considered as an "object." This is the "world as representation."

The principle of sufficient reason shapes this world's objective presentation, and Schopenhauer guides his exposition by referring to three of the principle of sufficient reason's four aspects that relate directly to this appearance. These are the relationships of necessary connection that hold between (1) material objects, (2) structures of space and time, and (3) abstract concepts. In Book II, Schopenhauer's discussion will consider what underlies the fourth, motive-focused, psychological aspect of the principle of sufficient reason, and will reveal the inner nature of physical objects in a dimension beyond the scientific view.

Book I also develops two related distinctions that reflect the object-centered forms of the principle of sufficient reason. These pairs run in parallel, and are "understanding versus reason" and "perceptual knowledge versus abstract knowledge." Schopenhauer describes the understanding as the source of perceptual knowledge, which is constituted by material objects, causality, space, and time. He describes reason as the source of abstract knowledge, which is constituted by abstract concepts. One of

Book I's main aims is to show how perceptual knowledge takes philosophical priority over abstract knowledge. Sections 1–7 focus on perceptual knowledge and the understanding. Sections 8–16 concern abstract knowledge and reason.

§§1–2: THE SUBJECT-OBJECT POLARITY AND KNOWLEDGE AS THE AWARENESS OF OBJECTS

The first line of *WWR* claims to express a foundational truth, namely, that "the world is my representation" ("*Die Welt ist meine Vorstellung*"). This is an unexpected assertion with which to begin, since it would not usually be said that the entire world is "my" representation. The usual view is that the world is an immense and complicated entity that encompasses far more than any one of us. It includes the earth, solar system, galaxies, and each person, leaf, pebble, blade of grass, grain of sand, chemical process, tiniest movement, etc., beyond any finite specification and beyond our comprehension.

Schopenhauer's way of beginning of *WWR* gives us a more immediate and personal perspective on things, as taken by someone who is perhaps sitting in a chair, wondering what the world is essentially like, and attempting to start his, her, or more importantly, "my" philosophizing from scratch, asserting most assuredly that right now, immediately before me, I apprehend a world. Insofar as I am an individual knowing subject, the world may be something beyond me, but in terms of my experience, it is fundamentally "my" world.

Taking a controversial step further, Schopenhauer reflects that the objects of his immediate awareness are his ideas, or "representations," and that these mental images, as such, depend upon his presence as a being that thinks, since mental images are entities that depend upon the mind within which they appear. This perspective interpretively transforms the world that a person apprehends, into his or her extensive set of mental images, thus supporting the phrasing of Schopenhauer's original proposition. He states accordingly that "the world is my representation," using the term "representation" to signify how his awareness of objects is constituted by his set of mental images. The world is the wealth of one's perceptions and memories. Schopenhauer adds mysteriously that "the world is my will"—a proposition that we will be able to understand only later—suggesting that the world is not simply an inanimate object, but is something importantly more.

Supporting this first-person characterization of the world, Schopenhauer asserts that in every instance, knowledge must be knowledge *for someone* or other. He is presently aware of, or "knows" a world that is being presented to him. By referring collectively and more expansively to everything that can be known as "the world," then insofar as it is known, that world, or object of knowledge, can exist only for some knower, that is, for some subject.

The upshot is that although all knowledge refers to some object, that knowledge also requires a subject who knows that object. Schopenhauer denies that there are known objects that exist on their own, mind-independently, for in that supposed condition we would be referring to mental images that have no relation to knowing subjects. Echoing Bishop George Berkeley's famous dictum, "to be is to be perceived," Schopenhauer maintains that to be an object of knowledge is identical to being known by some subject. At the foundation of knowledge, he consequently presents us with the subject-object distinction, where every object known requires a subject that is aware of it. As a slogan, he frequently states, "No object without a subject."[3]

Schopenhauer is careful to say that in Book I he is considering the world only as it appears as an object of knowledge, and as mentioned, he alludes to the presence of another side to the world. This is its inner dimension, which Schopenhauer establishes and describes in Book II as "will" or inner impulse, and as how the world is in itself. Book I analyzes the world's objective side, and Book II analyzes the world's subjective side. The objective side is the world's outer appearance; the subjective side is the world's inner reality. Schopenhauer will argue that the world's objective side depends upon its subjective side, analogous to how all objects of knowledge depend upon subjects for their being known. "No object without a subject" translates quickly to "no outer world without an inner world."

In a way, Schopenhauer's overall perspective is simple: he regards the world as a whole in just the way we naturally tend to regard our individual selves, namely, as being a body, like any other physical body, that is enlivened by an inner mind, or will. The inner mind underlies that body, but it is nowhere tangible, observable, or measurable within the scientific parameters of the physical body. One can slice, weigh, photograph, and scientifically examine a brain as much as one likes, but one will not find a consciousness to weigh. Yet the consciousness is there. By regarding the physical universe as structurally analogous to a conscious human body, it is a short step to posit an inner nature to the physical universe as a whole, its "mind," so to speak. Schopenhauer is delighted to discover this thought in the Upanishads, as it characterizes the world as having two sides, inner and outer, subjective and objective, called "Atman" and "Brahman" respectively.

Schopenhauer expresses these assorted ideas in §2 by saying that the subject is the supporter of the world and the universal condition of all that appears, adding that the subject knows all things but is known by none. This is puzzling, since humans are self-aware and speak about themselves as a matter of course. The odd phrasing stems from Schopenhauer's technical use of the word "know" as meaning "being presented in perception to consciousness *as an object*." If we think of ourselves as an object, then that conceptually frozen being we imagine cannot be the active and flowing consciousness that is doing the imagining. We nonetheless directly experience our feelings, sensations, and ideas, and have an awareness of ourselves as subjects. Only when we objectify those feelings into "things," the falsification occurs.

For Schopenhauer, subjects and objects are thus of different, though complementary, metaphysical kinds. He often uses the phrase "*toto genere* different" ("completely different in kind") to express the contrast. Self-awareness is possible, but whatever we are aware of in self-awareness, it cannot be an object of any kind, if we are to be directly aware of ourselves as active thinkers. Schopenhauer's image of the subject can be likened to an eye that can see other things, but cannot turn upon itself to see itself, just as a fingertip can touch other things, but cannot touch itself. The fingertip may not be able to touch itself, but the inside of the fingertip can be felt without touching anything. Self-awareness is of this latter kind.

Elaborating upon his conceptions of object and subject, Schopenhauer reiterates that the world's objective form has the qualities of space, time, and causality. He claims that the subject, on the other hand, is not in space or time. Like his technical definition of "knowledge" as exclusively the awareness of objects, Schopenhauer uses the term "subject" in a peculiar sense as well. He is not referring to the individual knowing subject, insofar as we are aware of ourselves here and now, but is referring to the timeless inner substrate that he believes underlies our spatial and temporal consciousness and that is the same in everyone. We will gain a better grasp of this idea in Book II, when Schopenhauer refers to this absolute reality that underlies everything as "Will."

It is worth recalling here how Schopenhauer adheres to Kant's idea that human nature as such, is both finite and rational. As an expression of our finite nature, Kant maintains that our experience must adhere to the forms of time and space. As an expression of our rational nature, Kant maintains that we must experience the world in terms of twelve conceptual categories that derive from elementary logic, among which he includes the category of causality. As we have noted, Schopenhauer rejects eleven of those twelve categories, retains the category of causality, and combines it with space and time to constitute the "understanding" as he wishes to define it. This is contrary to Kant, who defines the understanding exclusively in reference to the set of twelve conceptual categories, independently of space and time.

Kant regards the forms of space, time, and causality as knowable *a priori*, and as consequently universal and necessary for human experience. Since Schopenhauer is convinced that in his dissertation, *The Fourfold Root of the Principle of Sufficient Reason*, he demonstrated that all forms of necessity are encompassed by the principle of sufficient reason, he mentions here in §2 that in *WWR*, he will use the phrase "principle of sufficient reason" to include and to refer to all of the forms that Kant argues are knowable about the human mind independently of human experience and that operate as necessary conditions for our experience. In *WWR*, Schopenhauer thus uses the phrase "principle of sufficient reason" as shorthand for a joint reference to the forms of space, time, and causality—a triad that occurs often in *WWR*. Throughout all of this, both Kant and Schopenhauer regard the subject of experience as a being that is essentially timeless, since if the subject projects out of itself the form of time as a necessary condition for its experience, the subject cannot itself be at the point of projection, the very form it projects. It must be prior to the projection, and so it must be timeless and spaceless.

§3: TIME AND THE UNREALITY OF ORDINARY LIFE

Schopenhauer begins his philosophy by closely attending, as he says, to the "representation" (*Vorstellung*). The term "representation" can signify either the awareness of an individual thing or the thought of a concept. Schopenhauer accordingly partitions the field of representations into two groups, namely, intuitive and abstract. This follows the distinction between "intuitions" (*Anschauungen*) and "concepts" (*Begriffe*) that is elementary and crucial to Kant's theory of knowledge. Schopenhauer uses the terms "intuitive representations" and "abstract representations" in their place.

The set of abstract representations is constituted by our concepts, all of which Schopenhauer maintains we construct through a process of abstraction from perceptual experience. Saving his discussion of these for §8 and the sections following, he begins by characterizing the field of intuitive representations, which includes our ordinary perceptions of objects in addition to three of the fourteen conditions that for Kant, serve as the formal presuppositions for any experience. For Schopenhauer, as mentioned, these three are space, time, and causality. As also mentioned, these are the only three formal presuppositions that Schopenhauer recognizes, having dropped from consideration the remaining eleven categories of the understanding that Kant specified.

Drawing our attention to the "simplest" of these *a priori* conditions for experience, Schopenhauer considers the nature of time, and offers an analysis that has widespread implications throughout *WWR*. Arguing from the standpoint of the present moment, he observes that the past no longer exists and that the future does not yet exist. Like a dream, both are now unreal. Moreover, since the present is nothing more than the boundary between past and future—it is the dimensionless point of constant transition—it has no duration. So the present is also unreal. Everything experientially before us—past, present, and future—is thus without substance, like a dream.[4]

In a second argument for the unreality of time, Schopenhauer notes that since each moment is effaced by an upcoming moment, and since that upcoming moment will again be effaced by another, *ad infinitum*, the entire temporal sequence is self-effacing, and hence, unreal. This echoes how one can maintain that since any given event is contingent (since it could have been otherwise), the entire set of world events is contingent, and hence, stands either as an absurd and elementary fact, or as in need of some self-sufficient, noncontingent being to account for it.

In the spirit of these arguments, Schopenhauer states that with respect to their inherent dependency upon our own consciousness, all of the other forms of the principle of sufficient reason are of the same status as time, and hence, that ordinary life—the world of space and time, mathematics, geometry, causality, abstract concepts, and motives—is unreal, mirage-like, and akin to a grand perceptual illusion. The forms of the principle of sufficient reason provide only relative knowledge, and not absolute knowledge, and so the world they shape is endowed with only a relative kind of being. The world of representation is an illusion.

Enlisting support for the idea that the spatio-temporal world misrepresents how things truly are, Schopenhauer mentions a series of authoritative philosophers and philosophies who he interprets as expressing the same opinion, namely, Heraclitus, Plato, Spinoza, Kant, and the Upanishadic doctrine of *Maya*. Agreeing in the main with this group, Schopenhauer presents his own philosophical formulation as the most direct and perspicuous version of their shared perspective: the world of daily experience is an expanse of mind-dependent representations that, objectively speaking, is nothing more than a construction and artifact of the principle of sufficient reason. As a construction of our own mind, that world has no validity beyond the human sphere. Schopenhauer's position reiterates what Kant said of space and time, namely, that if we abstract from the human standpoint, then space and time stand for nothing whatsoever.[5]

§4: CAUSALITY AND MATTER

As §3 focuses on time, §4 discusses the nature of causality to continue Schopenhauer's exposition of the world's objective, spatio-temporal presentation. Causality is the projection of a necessary connection between events, and when Schopenhauer considers the notion of an event in greater depth, he observes that a concrete reference to causality presupposes a background fusion of space and time, that is, a spacetime continuum. Causality presupposes our awareness of an external world that contains the forms of material objects. Any material object maintains its distinctive shape over time, but it also changes from moment to moment. The object's constancy is due to its spatial quality, and the object's fluctuation is due to its temporal quality. The spatial and temporal dimensions together, as amalgamated in the object, lend the object its perceptual tangibility. This is why Schopenhauer states that "matter" (or better, the general form of it, or what one might call "matter in general") arises through the fusion of time and space, or in contemporary terms, through spacetime.

Causality involves specific variations in the happenings that take place at a particular time and place (e.g., the hammer's hitting the bell at noon caused a loud sound), and so it expresses the union of time and space in a concrete way. The notion of matter in general arises from the union of space and time, and the notion of matter with a set of specific qualities arises with the addition of causality to that union. Schopenhauer goes as far as to say that matter, understood in the concrete sense as being actively filled with a variety of qualities, is nothing but causality.

These reflections bear on Schopenhauer's reluctance to acknowledge the validity of the bulk of Kant's categories of the understanding, owing to his disposition to give philosophical precedence to intuitive knowledge as opposed to abstract knowledge. As we have noted, Schopenhauer rejects eleven of the twelve categories on the grounds that they are merely abstract concepts derived from perceptual experience. He now characterizes the remaining category of causality as the union of time and space according to a set of fixed rules. This does not reduce causality to that union (i.e., to matter in general), but Schopenhauer does integrate it inextricably with space and time, while

39

THE WORLD AS WILL AND REPRESENTATION

recognizing its intrinsic intellectual quality, namely, the idea of necessary connection as it bears lawfully between events. He concludes that *all perception is intellectually conditioned*, respecting how causality is rule-oriented in specific reference to material objects. We thus find Schopenhauer asserting that the world as representation exists only through the understanding, or "intellect," since causality is essential for that representation.

§5: THE MIND-DEPENDENT EXISTENCE OF THE EXTERNAL WORLD

Schopenhauer now applies some of the propositions he has established in the first four sections to the question of whether there is a mind-independent, external world—a world, or object, that would remain present if no perceivers were present. Schopenhauer denies that there is any such being. To begin, he reiterates that the principle of sufficient reason in any of its four specific applications is a principle that refers exclusively to how *objects* are, not to how subjects are. He has in mind a conception of the subject as a being that is, at bottom, independent of time and space.

Having argued that there can be no objects without subjects to be aware of them, if we acknowledge the presence of a world that is in space and time, and if we acknowledge that that world is a mental image, and has only a relative existence, then there must be some ground to this illusion that is not in space and time. For Schopenhauer, this is the unknowable "subject." For Kant, this is the unknowable "thing-in-itself."

Schopenhauer states that since the principle of sufficient reason applies only to relationships between objects, philosophical materialism makes no sense. This is because the materialist holds that our minds themselves come into existence by being *caused* by a previously existing material world or "object-in-itself." If, however, causality occurs only between *objects*, it would follow that a material object cannot cause a nonobject, or subject. Schopenhauer believes that the same inconsistency inhabits philosophical idealism insofar as it argues that our minds "cause" the material world, again objecting because causality holds only between objects.[6] Whatever key relationship holds between minds and material objects, it cannot be causality. Schopenhauer concludes that insofar as both materialism and idealism either appeal to or rest upon the concept of causality, both are mis-construed. He will reiterate this point in §7 below.

Schopenhauer resolves the conflict between materialism and idealism along Kantian lines by admitting initially that the "external world" is a set of representations that are connected objectively among themselves by the concept of causality, and that for this reason, that set of representations is fully deter-mined and hence, is perfectly predictable. In this respect, the external world is "empirically real," as Kant stated. It remains that since this set of representations requires our presence for its existence, the external world's being is "transcendentally ideal," where "ideal" means "relative to the human being's pres-ence," again, as Kant stated.[7] As such, life and dreams are leaves of one and the same book for Schopenhauer, and life, and with it, the deterministic world of mechanical causality, is essentially a long dream, or as we shall discover in Book II, a *nightmare*.

As far as the connection between mind and matter and the dispute between materialism and idealism is concerned, Schopenhauer introduces a new relationship that takes the place of causality. This is the relationship of "objectification" (*Objektivation*) or "manifestation" that allows for a difference, as well as an identity, between the mind and matter. For instance, ice cubes, steam, and liquid water each differ in appearance, but they are all manifestations of the same chemical substance, H_2O. In Book II, Schopenhauer will argue that the world of representation is the manifestation of a universal inner reality, the best word for which is "Will."

§6: OUR BODY AS OUR "IMMEDIATE OBJECT"

Schopenhauer observes that the starting-point for anyone's knowledge is the immediate consciousness of his or her pres-ence, as we noted above (§§1–2) in reference to the experience of feeling the inside of one's fingertip, independently of the fingertip's touching anything. Upon that starting point, one can then consider the sensations that arise when the fingertip does touch something. Perceptual objects are consequently constructed and are eventually understood as bearing causal relationships with each other.

The same applies to one's body as a whole. Through the immediate awareness of one's inner presence, there is an implicit awareness of one's body as such. Following upon the awareness of the accompanying sensations, there arises a more reflective and distinct awareness of one's body as an object located in space and time, that shares an environment with other objects, and that bears causal relationships to those objects.

Schopenhauer refers to the fundamental awareness of our presence as the awareness of our body as our "immediate object," using the term "object" in a rudimentary sense, independently of our self-consciously projecting cause-and-effect relationships. He has in mind the direct feelings that we have of our bodily states, such as when we apprehend our heartbeat, breathing movements, and inner feelings, purely and simply. In a more developed, precise, and technical sense, though, "objects" are the items that appear distinctly after the relationship of causality has been projected into our field of sensations, as when we distinguish our own body from the bodies of others.

Since animals share this kind of sensory awareness, and since he regards its intensity as being only a matter of degree, Schopenhauer maintains that the higher animals have understanding, or "intellect," and that it is structured in the same way as ours, namely, as an awareness of cause and effect relationships that hold between perceptual objects. Animals' perceptions are intellectually conditioned as well as ours. As illustrations, Schopenhauer refers to the sagacity of the elephant, monkey, and fox as examples of developed animal understanding. They do not have reason, that is, they do not form abstract concepts, but they do perceive cause and effect relationships with sharp discernment and intelligence.

§7: THE WORLD'S EXISTENCE IS MIND-DEPENDENT

Schopenhauer now reiterates his belief that his own philosophical method and style of argumentation differs from every other philosophy of which he is aware. Unlike materialist philosophies, he does not begin his argumentation by supposing a set of mind-independent objects, aiming to derive the existence of minds from them. Unlike idealist philosophies, he does not begin his argumentation supposing some original mind, or spirit, assumed to be independent of all objects, and aim to derive the existence of physical objects from the development of that original mind, or spirit. His arguments begin instead by supposing an original subject-object polarity—he refers to this as starting with the "representation" (i.e., mental image)—maintaining that this original polarity is at the basis of all explanation, and must therefore be presupposed at the outset. His argumentation starts with the root of the principle of sufficient reason, in other words, which is the condition for there being an awareness of anything specific at all.[8]

As noted above, Schopenhauer rejects philosophies that begin by assuming the existence of a set of supposedly mind-independent objects and which then try to derive consciousness from those objects. He believes that materialism is the most consistent of these attempts. The basic objects can also be abstract concepts, time, space, or God, considered as mind-independent beings. One of the problems Schopenhauer identifies is that these philosophies start with supposedly mind-independent objects that are *indirectly* given and are less well-known, and uses them to explain the presence of the mind that is directly given and much better-known—a mind that, moreover, posits those uncertain objects to begin with. Schopenhauer finds it absurd to explain what is immediately given and well-known in reference to what is indirectly given, and less well-known.

In the same vein, he rejects philosophies that start with an original mind or concept, and that aim to derive the physical world from that mind, as a spider spins a web. As noted above in specific reference to causality, Schopenhauer's objection to this—and his objection can be applied equally to those who wish to derive consciousness from matter—is that for the philosophies to work, it is necessary to presuppose the unrestricted universal application of the principle of sufficient reason. Only in this way can one derive, usually in terms of causality, matter from mind, or mind from matter, as a necessary implication. Owing to his acceptance of Kant's philosophy, Schopenhauer restricts the scope of the principle of sufficient reason exclusively to the realm of appearances. His objection is less with materialism or idealism *per se*, but with the use of causality as a metaphysical concept.

A fascinating segment of Schopenhauer's discussion is in his identification of a fundamental contradiction or "antinomy" in our faculty of knowledge. He recognizes how we can reason that a less complex state of matter from which human brains evolved, existed before the present time, and that an even less complex state of matter from which animal brains evolved existed before that, and that we can extend this logic back to some condition of primary matter, making it seem as if we have emerged as thinking beings from the increasing complexification of an originally given, elementary kind of matter. This is a common picture. Turning this sequence inside-out, Schopenhauer also recognizes that without first presupposing some minds to imagine that very sequence of material development, there would be nothing at all. The antinomy is that although my mind is in my head, my head is in my mind, and although my head is in my mind, my mind is in my head. This is a "strange loop" structure that has instances in a number of disciplines ranging from music, to the visual arts, to computer science.[9] Schopenhauer reveals its presence in the field of metaphysics, in connection with the relationship of mutual containment that obtains between materialism and idealism.

The result of Schopenhauer's discussion is to indicate that the inner nature of the world, or thing-in-itself, transcends the division between subject and object, along with the ceaseless transformation—like travelling along the surface of a Möbius strip—between subjective and objective standpoints inherent in the above antinomy. The inner nature of the world is the ground of the subject-object distinction itself, and it is not accessible through proofs or assertions of necessary connection of any kind, whether the connections obtain between concepts, material objects, mathematical or geometrical entities, or personal spiritual entities. Schopenhauer consequently maintains that the thing-in-itself is *toto genere* different from representations and the world of representations. If one is to gain access to the thing-in-itself, it will not be through a rational access and it will not involve any forms of the principle of sufficient reason. Book II will describe how a direct, intuitive access to the thing-in-itself is instead possible.

§8: PERCEPTUAL VS. CONCEPTUAL KNOWLEDGE

Schopenhauer now shifts his attention from the knowledge that direct perception provides, to what he refers to as the "borrowed light" from that perception. This borrowing involves the processes of "reflection" and "abstraction"—processes through which we construct abstract concepts from perceptual representations. We see a set of red things, for example, and construct the general concept "red" from the instances by reflecting upon them and isolating their salient visual quality. For Schopenhauer, all abstract concepts, as he uses the phrase, are empirical concepts. All abstract concepts are extracted from perceptual experience, and none are known *a priori*. Whenever we encounter the word "concept" in Schopenhauer's writings, which for him is synonymous with "abstract concept," we should mentally replace it with the term, "empirical concept."

Schopenhauer refers to our capacity for reflection as "reason," and asserts that reason has only one function, namely, to form abstract concepts. He maintains that the products of reason are less reliable than the immediacy of direct perception, and are a potential source of great error—error that can remain with us for centuries. At the same time, he recognizes that reason distinguishes us from the other animals, for it generates our plans and our principles, along with the capacity for deliberation and emotional control. Reason is consequently two-sided: while it takes us an uncertain step away from direct, perceptual knowledge and the certainty perceptual knowledge provides, reason's production of abstract knowledge elevates us above the animals by expanding the scope of our conscious awareness.

§§9–11: CONCEPTS AND LOGIC, AS OPPOSED TO FEELING

We now have in view two different classes of representations, namely, "abstract concepts" formed by reason, and "perceptual representations" formed by the understanding, in conjunction with space and time. Abstract concepts are conceived; perceptual representations are perceived.

Abstract concepts—the subject of this section—bear precisely specifiable relationships to each other. For example, (1) one concept can be included within another, as "horse" is contained within "animal";[10] (2) two concepts can partially intersect, as "dog" and "cat" share the concept of "four-legged"; (3) several concepts can be the species of a more general concept without overlap, as how triangles are defined by their angles, which are exclusively either "acute," "right," or "obtuse." From such elementary relationships derive the forms of judgment and forms of syllogistic reasoning.

Schopenhauer does not believe that the study of logic will help us reason better, for he holds that we have a natural capacity to grasp intuitively when a line of reasoning is valid or not. To discern what makes sense and what does not, there is no need to study a long inventory of valid and invalid logical forms beforehand. Similarly, he believes that studying aesthetics will not produce great artists, and that studying ethical theory will not produce anyone of great moral character. Logic nonetheless reveals the foundations of reason's workings and is informative in this regard.

Schopenhauer adds that the art of persuasion (i.e., rhetoric) is based on passing arbitrarily and selectively from one concept to another, closely associated concept, to create the *semblance* of implication—a semblance that can be used to win arguments. For instance, one can start with the concept of "passion" and associate it exclusively with the concept of "great force" (as when a person has a passion for some activity), but intentionally omit how passion is also sometimes associated with irrationality and weakness of rational capacities (as when a person is very passionate about something, but does not critically reflect upon it well, since he or she is "blinded" by the passion). By being misleadingly one-sided in this way, one can present a position more convincingly, showing only its attractive aspects.

Returning to his positive presentation of reason, Schopenhauer notes that although reason needs perceptual representations to produce abstract concepts, there are formal operations of reason that constitute a "pure science" of reason. These are expressed as principles of "metalogical" truth, and are the principles, or "laws" of (1) Identity: A is A, (2) Excluded Middle: A or not-A, and (3) Non-Contradiction: not both A and not-A. There is also the Principle of Sufficient Reason "of Knowledge," which concerns abstract concepts.[11] The first three are the familiar "laws of thought" that have been a part of Aristotelian logic for centuries.[12] The fourth Schopenhauer introduces from his doctoral dissertation.

In §11, there is a distinction between the abstract knowledge that reason produces and "everything else" that remains in consciousness, once we set aside all abstract knowledge. Schopenhauer calls this the sphere of feeling. It includes direct perception, what we ordinarily call "feelings," raw sensory pleasures and pains, awareness of one's power, weakness, contentment, as well as sophisticated religious feelings and reactions to great works of art. These feeling-related qualities of consciousness are all given in terms of direct apprehension and are not subject to logical proof.

§12: REASON VS. INTUITION IN PERFORMING WELL AND BEING GOOD

Schopenhauer notes that within the realm of feeling, where perceptual (or "intuitive") knowledge is the ground of all rational knowledge, perceptual knowledge nonetheless has its limitations. It is restricted, for instance, to what is immediately present. It attends to only the particular case. It is also unreflective. Rational knowledge has the advantage of being able to transform intuitive knowledge into a new, more usable, more communicative, more reproducible, and often more precise form, surpassing intuitive knowledge to that extent.

Schopenhauer prefers intuitive knowledge, though, for he notes that aside from rational knowledge's reliance upon it, intuitive knowledge is more effective in daily activity. The expert billiard-player, fencer, butcher, singer, musician, etc., is usually caught at a loss when reflecting too much on his or her activity. To perform excellently, it is optimal to be natural, automatic, and intuitive, even if that naturalness is based on years of technical training. A Zen archer is a perfect example.[13]

Schopenhauer also observes that sets of abstract concepts provide a discontinuous, mosaic-like representation of the continuously moving perceptual world, and that they falsify the world's appearance in that respect. Concepts introduce a stilted and mechanical quality to the interpretation of our surroundings, and do not serve well in artistic production. Concepts can guide artistic technique, but they are not the source of inspiration and artistic judgment. Book III develops this idea, wherein Schopenhauer maintains that genuine art issues from intuitive or perceptual knowledge.

Moreover, Schopenhauer ascribes to intuitive, as opposed to rational knowledge, what is essential to moral behavior, thus enhancing intuitive knowledge's value. Again, underscoring the importance of acting naturally, he finds immediate graciousness, friendliness, affection, etc., to be the most morally praiseworthy, as opposed to studied manners and proper behavior presented as if one were acting self-consciously from a textbook of social manners. In the same spirit, he associates virtue and holiness with feeling and inner depth, as opposed to reason. The latter may provide socially important rules such as "do not steal" and "honor thy father and mother," but according to Schopenhauer—and this is in direct conflict with Kant's moral theory—our self-awareness of being rational, and any respect we might have for ourselves as rational beings, has nothing to do with having a good will. Schopenhauer acknowledges some valuable ways in which reason enhances our consciousness, but on the most important issues concerning art, morality, and metaphysics, he subordinates reason to intuition.

§13: SCHOPENHAUER'S THEORY OF HUMOR

Schopenhauer now reflects upon the differences between abstract knowledge and perceptual knowledge that have been emerging in the preceding sections, and considers a noteworthy phenomenon that stems from our awareness of apprehending a certain kind of contrast between the two. He observes in particular that *laughter*, understood here as a humorous reaction to something, as opposed, say, to laughter that results from being tickled, rests upon our awareness of the distinction itself. He defines such laughter as a reaction to the incongruity between the actual condition of some actual object(s) and the way the object(s) is conceptually characterized. When there is an incongruity between perception and conception, we sometimes laugh. For instance, it can be funny to see an adult act like a child, a cat act like a dog, or a serious person act like a clown, owing to the incongruity between the behavior that is commonly defined as appropriate for that kind of person or being, and the behavior that is leading us to categorize the actor in a different category. In such cases, we have a person or thing (e.g., "adult") subsumed under a concept (e.g., "child") where the subsumption is paradoxical, inappropriate, or otherwise surprising.

In the second volume to *WWR*, Schopenhauer states in chapter VIII, "On the Theory of the Ludicrous," that everything ludicrous results from a particular kind of reasoning where one begins with an undisputed major premise, adds an unexpected minor premise, and draws a laughable conclusion. Consider a person known to be a highly intelligent, musical genius, who when laughs, giggles with a silliness expressive of an empty and superficial spirit, as Mozart was portrayed in the film, *Amadeus*. The syllogism would be: M is a highly intelligent, serious, musical genius, M tends to giggle, therefore serious geniuses giggle. It is, though, difficult to squeeze every instance of humor into such a syllogistic form.

Schopenhauer also describes humor as involving the subsumption of an object under a concept where the object is congruent with the concept for the most part, except for an outstandingly incongruous quality that causes the humorous reaction. Some versions of the incongruity theory might be the most effective in accounting for humor, but it should be said that if accurate, Schopenhauer would at best be identifying a necessary, but not sufficient condition for humor. There are non-humorous instances of incongruous qualities that involve sadness or pity, as when an otherwise virtuous person is ruined by some fatal flaw or weakness.[14]

§§14–15: PERCEPTUAL KNOWLEDGE AS THE BASIS OF SCIENCE, MATHEMATICS, AND GEOMETRY

Schopenhauer has been distinguishing rational knowledge from intuitive knowledge along several dimensions, and this section concerns another advantage that rational knowledge provides, namely, the formulation of scientific laws. Schopenhauer states that a "science" of some given subject matter aims to assemble a complete abstract knowledge of that subject. This involves a systematic arrangement of the conceptual knowledge that is both fully unified under a single principle (respecting the "law of homogeneity") and fully specified into as many levels of diversity as appropriate (respecting the "law of specification"). A perfect "system" has maximal unity and maximal diversity.

Even if one were to achieve a scientific knowledge of some subject matter, Schopenhauer emphasizes once more that this abstract knowledge traces back to, and is grounded upon, direct perceptual knowledge. To move from the perceptual knowledge to the abstract knowledge—to understand the relevant features of perceptual knowledge that are relevant to formulating scientific laws—the power of judgment is required. Schopenhauer, echoing Kant, accordingly maintains that "judgment" is the intermediary between "understanding" and "reason." His main point is to highlight how scientific knowledge is only a summary of perceptual knowledge, and that the latter is what we should always respect as philosophically and experientially basic.

Developing this idea in §15, Schopenhauer reflects upon the nature of mathematics and geometry, and argues that a rationalistic or reason-based understanding of these disciplines is misguided.[15] His target is Euclid, who is known for his axiomatic, rationalistic presentation of geometry: starting with self-evident definitions and axioms, Euclid uses logical deduction to extend the content of these definitions and axioms into theorems and further propositions. Schopenhauer's leading objection to this Euclidean approach is that it is too mechanical, and does not provide genuine understanding: by using mere definitions and logic, one cannot directly "see," for example, that the sum of the areas of the squares formed by the legs of a right triangle equals the area formed by the square of the hypotenuse. We know "that" the areas are equal, but we do not know "why." With the simple diagram, however (Schopenhauer provides the diagram in the text for this example), we can directly perceive these relationships.

It is fair to say that Schopenhauer tends to be unsympathetic with purely logical or rationalistic methods, as we can see further from his criticisms of Spinoza and Fichte. To the contrary, he often reiterates—especially in this first Book—that perceptual knowledge takes precedence over abstract knowledge, and that when it comes to truth and to philosophy, perception trumps conception.

One might ask how Schopenhauer can maintain that perceptual, as opposed to conceptual, methods should prevail in geometry and mathematics, when it seems clear that logical inference is substantial to both disciplines. Against those who would argue that geometry and mathematics are nothing more than extensions of symbolic logic, Schopenhauer invokes Kant's distinction between "forms of sensibility" and "concepts of the understanding." The former exhaustively include space and time; the latter, for Kant, exhaustively include the twelve categories of the understanding that he derived from the elementary forms of logical judgment.

Having Kant's notion of space in view, Schopenhauer grounds his attack on Euclid upon the supposition that we can have, or come very close to, a "pure perception" of space or time, devoid of any content. He believes that we can imagine the pure containers themselves, along with their inherent mathematical and geometrical structures, into which our sensory inputs flow. It is not logic that operates here, but reflection upon the pure perceptions of space and time.

To grasp this kind of "pure perception," imagine that we are driving along a crowded highway. Then imagine less cars on the road, one by one, and then further imagine the road and the landscape not being there, continuing with this thought experiment to remove *everything* sensory, including the distant stars. This removal of "empirical perception" leaves us, supposedly, with two pure perceptions *a priori*, which take the form of transparent containers, namely space and time, whose structures we can independently examine. For Schopenhauer, this direct apprehension of the pure intuitions of space and time is the basis for mathematical and geometrical awareness, and it accentuates how he upholds perception—in this case pure perception—over any kinds of conceptualization, understood as the formation of concepts from the contents of empirical perception.

Moving from geometry and mathematics to natural science, Schopenhauer advances the same claim against natural science that he advances against Euclid's style of understanding geometry: science does not give us the "why," but only explains "that" events are sequenced in certain patterns. Scientific explanations remain on the surface of things, for they explain the relationships between objects in mechanical, causal terms, and conclude inevitably with non-explainable forces that are simply given. To Schopenhauer, this inadequacy of scientific explanation indicates that there is an inner nature to things that science cannot touch. At this point, scientific explanation reaches its end, and philosophical explanation begins.

§16: PERCEPTUAL KNOWLEDGE AT THE BASIS OF VIRTUE AND LIVING WELL

In this concluding section to Book I, Schopenhauer addresses "practical reason," that is, reason's application in daily activity. He appreciates the power that reason gives us over less-developed animal consciousnesses, and observes how the dramatic advantage that animals with eyes have over those without them, compares to the great advantage that humans, who have reason, have over all other animals. Animals that are sightless have a limited grasp of the wider expanse of space that surrounds them, whereas animals with eyes can see that wider expanse directly and in detail. Yet all animals, with eyes or without them, have a limited grasp of the expanse of time that surrounds them, as it extends infinitely into the past and future, and hence, they live almost entirely in the present and lack a conception of their upcoming deaths. Humans, who possess reason, are aware of time's expanse beyond the present moment, and are consequently aware of their upcoming deaths. Schopenhauer ascribes understanding to animals, and as constituents of the understanding, space, time, and causality, but only in the presence of reason do the structures of these forms emerge clearly.

Despite the power that reason provides, Schopenhauer continues to resist rationalistic views that regard reason as the means to resolve either metaphysical problems or problems related to how we ought to live. With respect to the latter, reason appears to be neutral. For example, a person can distance himself or herself from a situation using reason, and can make detailed and forceful plans. The plans, however, could have little or no moral content, as Schopenhauer believes is true for deliberate plans that involve suicide, executions, and duels. Extremely high intelligence in an evil person works in the service of evil to exemplify "rational action," but not "virtuous action."

On a potentially more promising note, Schopenhauer speaks of the Stoics who professed to live according to reason in view of a virtuous ideal. This important discussion prepares us for the rest of *WWR*, for Schopenhauer observes in Stoic ethics a set of qualities that he will incorporate within his own view. He agrees that reflection upon a given situation can produce a feeling of psychological detachment and a consequent feeling of tranquillity. He agrees that the final goal is peace of mind, or inner tranquillity. He agrees that happiness is related to the proportion between what we want and what we receive; if we want much less, then we are likely to be relatively more happy. He also agrees that no satisfaction is permanent, that the world is in constant flux, and that detachment from both jubilation and sorrow is a means to happiness. Many of the Stoic goals appear in Schopenhauer's view; the difference resides in Schopenhauer's alternative way to realize them.

The Stoic sage who would embody the above ideas by using reason, comes under criticism as being wooden, stiff, and lacking in poetical truth. This is consistent with the often-encountered meaning of the word "stoic," as when one assumes a stoic, emotionally unmoved reaction to the death of a loved one. Schopenhauer believes a compassionate attitude is more enlightened and that attitudes of indifference that harden the heart, do not provide a genuine or pure peace of mind, but only an empty tranquillity.

Schopenhauer also criticizes the Stoics for believing that a pain-free condition within ordinary life is possible. Schopenhauer maintains that to live, is *thereby* to suffer from the frustrations that desire produces, and that only by denying life in some sense— by denying our natural desires—can we achieve a genuine tranquillity. For him, the idea of living without suffering is contradictory. In Book IV, Schopenhauer will explore this idea of denying our natural desires for the sake of inner tranquillity.

As an alternative to the Stoics, Schopenhauer points toward sages from other traditions whose views are consistent with the bulk of the Stoic's ethical insights, but who acknowledge life's inherent suffering. He mentions sages from India, but as the person with highest significance and as embodying the greatest poetic truth, Schopenhauer refers us to Jesus, who he describes as embodying a condition of supreme suffering, while retaining perfect virtue, holiness, and sublimity. This is one of the many Christian images that appear in *The World as Will and Representation*.

STUDY QUESTIONS

1. Unlike materialists who begin their philosophizing by assuming the existence of mind-independent objects, and unlike idealists who begin their philosophizing by assuming

the existence of an object-independent subject, how does
Schopenhauer begin his philosophizing?
2. Explain why Schopenhauer defines "knowledge" exclusively
   in terms of one's having an awareness of "objects." Does this
   mean that "self-knowledge" is impossible?
3. Explain how Schopenhauer gives prominence to perceptual
   knowledge (i.e., intuitive knowledge) over abstract knowledge
   (i.e., conceptual knowledge) in the following areas: (1) in his
   critique of Euclid, (2) in his critique of Stoic ethics, (3) in
   his critique of rationalistic philosophy, as in the views of
   Spinoza and Fichte.
4. Describe how Schopenhauer uses the distinction between
   perceptual knowledge and abstract knowledge to explain
   humor.

SECTION 3. BOOK II, WILL AS THING-IN-ITSELF, §§17–29

§17: THE SUPERFICIALITY OF MATHEMATICS, GEOMETRY, NATURAL SCIENCE, AND OBJECT-BASED PHILOSOPHY

Turning now toward the world as "the objectification of Will,"
Schopenhauer begins Book II by reiterating how his philosophy
focuses on the prime constituents of our experience, or upon
"the representation" (mental image), and with this, he continues
to develop the theme that arises at the end of Book I, namely,
whether science can provide any direct insight into the nature of
things-in-themselves. This is to ask whether scientific awareness
can constitute metaphysical awareness and by doing so, occupy
the historical position that philosophy has enjoyed for centuries.
Schopenhauer's conception of the metaphysical quest involves
searching for the essential content of the representation, for
example, we see a tree, or a chair, or a stone, or the sun, or our
body, and wonder what its nature happens to be, if what we
ordinarily perceive does not exhaust the nature of what is. It is a
response to the question of whether the perceptual world is anything *more*, or anything deeper, or anything more significant,
than sequences of fleeting mental images and memories. In this
section, Schopenhauer considers some of the paths that have
been taken traditionally to understand the nature of what
we experience, or what he would term the essential nature of the

representation, and he rejects them all. These are the methods of abstract ideas, mathematics, natural science, and naturalistic philosophy, where the concept of causation predominates.

Schopenhauer appreciates that there is a sense in which abstract concepts can provide a more concise presentation of perceptual representations' content insofar as abstract concepts coalesce, condense, and simplify the perceptual representations' meaning into single concepts. Since abstract concepts only summarize the field of perceptual representations, though, they do not go beyond what the perceptual representations themselves offer. They do not consequently illuminate the metaphysical meaning of the perceptual field, but only represent it more summarily, schematically, and usefully.

Traditional philosophy also tries to reveal the nature of perceptual representations. Schopenhauer has here in mind philosophy that is based on the concept of causality, as in philosophies that refer to God as the "uncaused cause" of the world, or that refer to physical objects as the cause of our ideas. Such philosophy typically starts with the assumption that perceptual representations such as the earth, trees, and so on, are mind-independent objects, causally connected to one other. Schopenhauer rejects this understanding of the world, reiterating his arguments in Book I to the effect that there are no mind-independent objects to begin with. He assumes fundamentally that all objects are mental images, and as such, depend upon a subject for their being.[16]

Neither does Schopenhauer believe that mathematics can reveal the inner nature of representations, since mathematics refers only to quantities related to representations' spatial and temporal form. Following Kant, Schopenhauer maintains that geometry (much of which can be translated into mathematics) and mathematics derive respectively from the structures of space and time. Since Schopenhauer accepts the Kantian position that space and time are not features of things-in-themselves, he accordingly denies that mathematics can provide metaphysical insight. The discipline is too superficial and describes only how things-in-themselves appear, not how they are in themselves, as complete as such a description of the appearances might be.

Operating on the same superficial plane of appearances, natural science is based on the concept of causality, and as we have seen Schopenhauer argue in Book I, the concept of causality, status-wise, compares to the forms of space and time. As an aspect of the principle of sufficient reason, causality is a human-relative notion, expressive of how we must experience the world, and not, as far as we can know, how the world is in itself. It consequently has no power to reflect the nature of things-in-themselves, that is, the metaphysical nature of representations. When it does try to provide such insight, it steps beyond its sphere of proper application.

Schopenhauer concludes from this initial survey that traditional philosophy, mathematics, geometry, abstract ideas, and natural science cannot answer the philosophical question of what the nature of the world happens to be. Natural science can explain how events are structured in relation to each other, but these scientific explanations eventually arrive at, or simply presuppose, natural forces whose inner nature remains mysterious.

The implication is soon obvious: *we can not get at the inner nature of things by observing the outer qualities of things.* We cannot get at a thing's subjectivity by regarding that thing as an object. Stated in more technical terms, we cannot become aware of the inner nature of things by invoking the principle of sufficient reason in any of its forms, for those forms are precisely the forms of abstract concepts, mathematics, geometry, and causality, where causality is understood exclusively to involve relationships between objects. All natural science and any traditional philosophy that is based on the concept of causality is fated, so to speak, to hit fruitlessly against a wall, when it comes to revealing the answers to metaphysical questions.

There is a terminological complication in Schopenhauer's discussions, since he usually uses the term "knowledge" (*Erkenntniß*) to refer exclusively to knowledge of objects. The idea of "metaphysical knowledge" would thus be a contradiction in terms, if the aim of metaphysics is to provide an insight into the nature of things—an insight to be gained not by observing some object from the outside, but by coinciding with the object's inner reality. One would more consistently speak of "metaphysical insight," where "insight" is a term that allows a reference to whatever we become aware of when we directly apprehend the inner nature of things.

This would not be "knowledge" on Schopenhauer's view, strictly speaking. Given this technical use of the term "knowledge" as "knowledge of objects," he can consistently say that knowledge of the thing-in-itself is impossible, or that metaphysical knowledge is impossible. The words seem to express Kant's view, but it would be an interpretive mistake to accept this verbal appearance and read Schopenhauer as a Kantian who believes that we have no access to the thing-in-itself. Neither the claim that "knowledge" of the thing-in-itself is impossible, nor the claim that metaphysical "knowledge" is impossible implies for Schopenhauer that we cannot have a metaphysical insight into the nature of the thing-in-itself. It is easy to become confused by this, and believe mistakenly that because Schopenhauer's discussions sometimes suggest that knowledge of the thing-in-itself is impossible, he is a Kantian who precludes from having any knowledge *or* direct insight into the thing-in-itself.

In subsequent sections, Schopenhauer speaks loosely of a "double knowledge" that we have of our bodies, as in §19, and in §18, of the "knowledge" of ourselves as will. It would have been more exact for him to have said "double apprehension" or "double awareness" to avoid conflict with his technical use of the term "knowledge." The present exposition will aim to use the term "knowledge" in Schopenhauer's more restricted, technical sense as much as possible, and to use alternative terms such as "awareness" or "apprehension" or "insight" when the discussion refers to the inner nature of things.

§18: THE DOUBLE AWARENESS OF OUR BODIES

Moving now toward a positive answer to the question of what underlies our field of representations—an answer that will bring us to the "inside" of things, as opposed to the externalistic methods outlined in the previous section—Schopenhauer offers one of his main arguments in support of the general idea that the inner nature of the world is best referred to as "Will."[17] He is searching for a way to grasp the inner nature of the field of representations, having realized that all external methods fail to break through to the inside. He is looking at the cup of coffee on his table, for instance, and is trying to discern a way to be "inside" the cup of coffee, so he can apprehend its metaphysical being. This, he believes, is what genuine philosophy seeks. He finds the key in his direct apprehension of his own body and discovers, in effect, that he is *already* on the inside of one of the representations within his field of perceptual representations.

Schopenhauer observes that insofar as it is a physical object, his body is just the same as any other physical object. The representation has a shape, occupies a specific area of space, endures through time, and has a weight, density, three-dimensionality, and perceptual tangibility in its coloration that compares with any other physical object. To a surgeon, a body is a physical object that reacts like other physical objects. To me, your body as such, as you stand beside me, is a physical object like the chair or table here with us. My body appears the same way to you. Both of our bodies occupy a part of my visual field like the other objects I see, and as an object *per se*, my own body appears to me as being of the same kind as all of the other objects in my perceptual field. Appreciating how Schopenhauer apprehends his body as just another physical object—just another representation—among the billions of physical objects in the world, metaphysically no different, better, worse than any of the others, is central to understanding his main argument.

Given how our bodies, considered as physical objects, are identical in kind with every other object in the physical world, Schopenhauer asks us to notice something metaphysically important: we each have a special relationship to our bodies, for we are on the "inside" of our bodies and can feel them like no other physical body. We pick up a cup of coffee to drink, and feel the inside of our hand, but do not feel the inside of the cup or of the coffee. And yet, the hand, the cup and the coffee are equally objects that are being perceived.

Schopenhauer concludes crucially that we experience our body in two different ways. As he says, we have a "double knowledge" (*doppelte Erkenntniß*) of it: we can observe it as we can observe any other physical object, as when we look in the mirror or hold up our hand; we can also feel our body from the inside and thus, quite unlike the position of every other being, have a direct awareness of our body. One's body is given in intelligent perception as a "representation," and hence as an object, just like any other object. One's body is also given as being under one's direct control. We feel, move, shape, and express ourselves through our bodies, as we apprehend—or rather, as we "are"—our body from the inside.

Schopenhauer's primary observation and philosophical claim is that these two aspects of our bodies, "the inner" and "the outer," are metaphysically the *same* being. They are two sides of a coin. They are essentially the same reality presenting itself in different ways. An act of will and the corresponding bodily movement are, for him, the same. The act of will does not "cause" the movement, as if the willing could be separated from the movement, assuming to the contrary that the two were metaphysically distinct. The act and its manifestation are identical, just as "electricity" and a bolt of lightning are identical.

Expanding upon this idea, Schopenhauer states that our will, considered as a whole, is therefore objectively visible as our bodies. If we examine our bodies carefully, he believes, we can perceive the manifestation of our inner being. Conversely, if we knew what we essentially were, we would understand why we appear as we do. External form is the manifestation of inner being. Every impression on the body is thereby an impression upon the will. When the quality of the impression coincides with the will's nature and aims, we experience pleasure; when the quality of the impression conflicts with the will's nature and aims, we experience pain.

Schopenhauer intends this double-aspect view to provide a more coherent alternative to mind-body causal interaction, as when one might say according to the latter, that my willing causes my hand to rise, or that my desire to satisfy my thirst causes me to pick up a glass of water. Rather, my hand rising is my willing objectified, and my picking up of the glass is my desire to satisfy my thirst objectified. A consequence of Schopenhauer's discussion of the principle of sufficient reason is that causal relationships obtain only between *objects*, so his theory does not permit references to physical conditions that cause mental conditions. He consequently needs to find other locutions that describe the situation. To do this, he renders the subject and object metaphysically identical, and speaks of a condition on one side of the distinction being immediately manifested on the other side, as the movements of a hand within a glove are immediately evident and are the same as the motions of the gloved hand, as when an external observer sees only the glove moving.

One of the most threatening problems for Schopenhauer's argument arises in connection with his insistence that the knowledge of one's will and the knowledge of one's physical body as such, are inseparable, owing to their metaphysical identity. A difficulty arises from how we are aware of our inner impulses, or will, only as we engage in some bodily activity at this or that time. Schopenhauer says explicitly that we cannot have any awareness of ourselves as willing beings without our *also* having an awareness of our bodies. At the very least, this implies that our direct awareness of ourselves as "will" always occurs *in time*.

If our awareness of ourselves as "will" always occurs in time, and if time is a form of the principle of sufficient reason, as Schopenhauer has argued in line with Kant's philosophy, then our awareness of ourselves as "will" is conditioned by the principle of sufficient reason. This is the problem. As such, it cannot be an absolute awareness that reveals the true, inner nature of the representations.

Schopenhauer thus appears to have created a dilemma for himself by emphasizing the priority of perceptual experience over abstract knowledge, or any other kind of knowledge. Once perceptual experience is regarded as fundamental, and once it is admitted that all perceptual experience happens in time, then it would seem that metaphysical insight, or insight about the nature of the thing-in-itself is ruled out, if time is a form of the principle of sufficient that can only present appearances of the thing-in-itself, rather than offer any direct and fully revelatory awareness of it.[18]

This appears to be a strong objection to Schopenhauer's argument and foundation of his philosophy, but Schopenhauer has a reasonable response: he states that insight into the nature of the thing-in-itself is a matter of degree. We might not have a complete and absolute insight, but we can come very close indeed, as we apprehend the thing-in-itself through, as he says, the "thin veil" of time. This is far from the Kantian view that insight into the nature of the thing-in-itself is impossible.

In the above, Schopenhauer uses the metaphor of "veils" that "cover" the thing-in-itself, and it is important to appreciate that this metaphor is only an expression of Schopenhauer's argument, rather than the argument itself. Contrary to Schopenhauer's use of the notion, there are some instances of "veils" where their combination does not obscure the object veiled, but renders the object more clear, as when two colored filters in conjunction, yellow and blue, provide a better image of an object's color, than does a single blue filter.[19] This example makes no difference to Schopenhauer's own argument, however, for the argument is that we have three main "veils" that obscure the thing-in-itself, namely, causality, space, and time, and that the removal of causality and space will reveal the thing-in-itself more clearly. The reason is that the thing-in-itself is an "inner" apprehension, and is obscured by the more outer-oriented forms of causality and space. That time is the form of inner experience coincides more with the nature of the thing-in-itself as Will. So it is not the formal presence of "veils" and the logic of their removal that supports Schopenhauer's argument, but the way in which, among the three fundamental forms of our experience, time is the form of inner experience, as opposed to the two other forms.

It remains that one could argue that the presence of *any* form of the principle of sufficient reason is sufficient to preclude all insight into the nature of the thing-in-itself. We only need one form to push us back to the Kantian position, and that we happen to have three forms, only overdetermines a problematic situation.

In response to this stronger argument, it helps to recall that in §3, Schopenhauer describes "the present" as a dimensionless point that marks the boundary between an unreal past and unreal future. This description is now applicable revealingly within the present context. Although the apprehension of one's inner being as "will" always takes place in the present, one's apprehension of this present can range between an exclusive attention to the present moment, and a highly expanded attention to the "past-present-future" continuum. At the extremes, two conceptions of time emerge, namely, the "eternal now," as opposed to the more mathematical, and Kantian, conception of time as a continuum that extends from the past, through the present, and into the future. If one's present awareness is not highly projective into the past or future, and if one remains focused on the "now," then a more timeless awareness will follow—one that is more conducive to apprehending the presence of the thing-in-itself as "Will." It is the Kantian conception of time that gets in the way, rather than the more diaphanous eternal "now."

Schopenhauer concludes this section by stating that the direct apprehension of the identity of the will and the body—the direct apprehension that "the inner" and "the outer" aspects of our body are the same—is a "miracle" and philosophical truth *par excellence*. He grounds his philosophy upon the direct apprehension of this identity. Once it has been established that his body is the objectivity of his will, the identity can be extended to assert that the world as representation (i.e., considering the world upon analogy to the human body) is the objectivity of "Will," where the latter is taken as the absolute and universal inner being of everything.

§19: THE KEY TO THE INNER BEING OF EVERY REPRESENTATION

Now that Schopenhauer has established that there is a double-apprehension, double-awareness, or "double knowledge," as he says, of one of the representations within his perceptual field, namely, the representation of his body, he asks a question about the other representations, since with this inner access to one of his representations, he feels that he has discovered the key to the inner nature of all representations. For either some or all of the other representations have no inner reality, and are not like the representation of which Schopenhauer has a double-awareness, or they all do have an inner reality, and are like the representation of which Schopenhauer has a double-awareness.

With respect to his field of perceptual representations, which to him seems at first like an impenetrable wall in its flat objectivity, Schopenhauer reasons that if no other representations have an inner reality aside from that of his body, then he (or anyone else performing this thought-exercise, as it would seem to that person) would be the only being in existence that has an inner reality. This is the position of theoretical egoism, or solipsism, which maintains that "only I exist."

Schopenhauer rejects this position as unlikely, since among all of the representations in his perceptual field, he does not perceive the representation of his body *qua* representation as being at all special or perceptually distinguished. It appears to be a representation exactly like any other, as it is spatially contiguous with other representations, just as others are contiguous with yet others, and so there is no apparent reason why there should be any exceptions to the idea that every representation has an inner reality. If there were exceptions, the perceptual field would present itself as absurd, where among a set of equally full-fledged, waking-state representations, some would have inner realities and some would not, inexplicably.

Such reflections lead Schopenhauer to conclude that every representation in his visual field has an inner reality, just as the representation that is his body has an inner reality. Upon reaching this point, we are approaching the position that there is a *single* inner reality behind the entire field of perceptual representations, of which Schopenhauer's (and everyone else's) consciousness is an expression. We will see why shortly.

It is possible to interpret Schopenhauer's argument as an "argument from analogy," since he says that he will judge all other representations which are not our own body, upon "analogy" (*Analogie*) to how our body is given to us in a double sense, namely, as representation and as will. If so, it is easy to criticize it as a weak argument, since we are projecting from only one instance to innumerably many instances. A strong argument from analogy would run in the other direction: since after having experienced, say, 20,000 examples of some item, each of which has 15 salient qualities, if we were to encounter another item that has 14 of those qualities, we could infer by analogy that the 15th quality is likely to be present as well. Schopenhauer has no argument of this structure, however.

Schopenhauer is not intending to advance an "argument from analogy" in the above-stated format. His argument is based on identifying the conditions required for making sense of a given phenomenon, which in this case is the perceptual field that contains a variety of representations. The argument is that if (1) we know through *direct awareness* that one of the representations has an inner nature, and (2) that *qua* representation, the representation we apprehend as having an inner nature is not obviously special (e.g., the body of another person sitting at the dinner table, is just as much of a physical object as are the knives, forks, cups, plates, food, flowers, and candles; the body takes up space, moves, makes sounds, has a texture, gives off heat, etc.), then (3) if we do not suppose that all of the other representations have an inner nature of the same kind, then the perceptual field will be less philosophically coherent than if we suppose that they do.

If we follow Schopenhauer, and admit that all of the other representations in our visual field have an inner reality, the "analogy" to which he refers arises in more of its own right at the subsequent level, namely, it arises in supposing that, given that all of the other representations have an inner nature, that inner nature is the same, or is roughly the same (i.e., analogous), as the inner nature of the representation of which we are in direct contact. The referred-to analogy does not establish *that* other representations have an inner nature. The analogy enters into the argument when we consider *what* that inner nature is like in the other representations.

Schopenhauer might be understood to be assuming, rather unconvincingly, that we cannot imagine any other kind of inner nature than what we experience in ourselves as "will," and so whatever the inner nature of the other representations happens to be, since all representations *qua* representation are the same, it has to be roughly the same as our own. There is, however, a stronger reason to regard the inner nature of all other representations as "will." If notions of diversity and multiplicity are restricted to the field of representations in relation to their nature as objects, that is, if attributions of multiplicity remain in the realm of the principle of sufficient reason, then with respect to the representations' subjective side, there will be no multiplicity. It follows that there can be only one inner nature that underlies all representations. This is the key idea that allows Schopenhauer to refer to the "Will" as a single being that manifests itself equally in all of us.

It remains that once any philosophy moves into the specifics of what our inner reality is—Schopenhauer calls it "will"—there is room for disagreement. Some individuals who meditate discover not "will," but a placid "clear light," others encounter a blissful and infinitely expanded consciousness, others experience the sheer flow of time, others discover the structure of self-consciousness. This requires us to examine Schopenhauer's rationale for describing his self-apprehension specifically as "will," keeping in mind these other candidates. He is aiming to provide a characterization of our inner being whose basic quality is capable of explaining what we perceive before us in ordinary experience. How the perceptual field with all of its inherent violence could be understood as the manifestation of a clear light, or of a field of bliss, presents an incredible mystery. How it could be understood as the manifestation of a blind Will is less puzzling, as Schopenhauer will show.

§20: THE OBJECTIFICATION OF WILL

Schopenhauer is convinced that he has correctly identified the inner reality of our bodies, and of all representations, as "will," and he states that this will is immediately noticeable in our voluntary actions, as when we act to raise our arm or turn our head. As mentioned, he does not say that the act of will "causes" the arm to raise or the head to turn. For him, the inner act and the outer behavior are two sides of the same coin, and it compares to saying that "electricity," considered generally, "manifests" itself as sparks, lightning, glowing wires, and such. Electricity does not cause the sparks or the lightning bolts; it "is" the sparks and the bolts.

Describing human activity is more complicated, since in addition to the fundamental act of will that appears behaviorally, there are also motives that drive a person's action, for example, to bring fresh air into the room, one opens the window. The motives provide the reason for the action, but the inner reality that the action itself is, is metaphysically independent of any motives. The motives are like the physical conditions that determine whether electricity will manifest itself as a spark or as a lightning bolt in this or that situation; the sparks and bolts themselves differ from whatever external conditions (atmospheric moisture, heat, pressure, etc.) have made them into sparks or bolts at that time and place. Schopenhauer thus distinguishes the inner reality, or "will," as groundless and independent of the principle of sufficient reason and its various expressions, which include motives.

Assuming that an act and its behavioral manifestation are metaphysically one and the same, Schopenhauer observes that we can refer to acts at different levels of generality. There can be an act defined in terms of some action that takes place at a specific point in time, as in the above example of opening the window to let in some fresh air. There can also be an act that is defined more generally as the way a person is, that is, as the expression of the person's more general character. One might say, for instance, "Jane is an honest character; she tells the truth."

Schopenhauer refers to a person's fixed, universal, and timeless character quality as his or her "intelligible" character. The historical expression of this intelligible character through a set of motives, he calls the person's "empirical character." This leads Schopenhauer to maintain that a person's body is the expression of his or her intelligible character, which is the core act of will that the person is. By reflecting upon our respective patterns of motivations that structure our empirical character, we can discern to some extent, what our intelligible character is. A person might be driven fundamentally by the quest for pleasure, or for recognition, fame, tranquillity, friendship, security, money, competition, power, etc., and this drive, or a constellation of drives, would structure the person's intelligible character. Once that person is born into a specific historical situation, specific structures of motivations relative to the historical situation will arise that define an empirical character: François-Xavier aspires to be one of Napoleon's generals; Plato aspires to be one of Socrates's students; Valentina aspires to be an astronaut.

Insofar as we can understand our inner, personal character as a fundamental act of will, Schopenhauer maintains that this character displays itself in our bodies as a whole. If we examine a person's body, we can see their character manifested. At a certain level, and following the analogy to electricity mentioned above, he believes that a person's body "is" their character. In this respect, he states that my body is nothing but my will having become visible. This proposition can only be understood in general terms, though, since it is obvious that people's bodies frequently have outward appearances that are due to accidental events.

Expanding upon this style of interpretation, and doing so in appropriately generic terms, Schopenhauer adds that (1) the human form is the objectified human will; it is the will of "humanity" objectified, (2) the teeth, gullet and intestinal canal are objectified hunger, (3) the genitals are objectified sexual impulse, (4) grasping hands and nimble feet are the objectified desires that in the case of humans, involve, presumably, tool-making, building, linguistic gesturing, running, and so on. In each instance, Schopenhauer observes a physical structure or phenomenon and regards it as the expression of some inner impulse, barring accidentally formed structures, as when a person walks with a limp owing to having been injured accidentally by a passing vehicle. Schopenhauer is speaking of naturally occurring structures and behaviors.

§21: THE INNER NATURE OF ALL REPRESENTATIONS IS "WILL"

As we have seen, Schopenhauer argues in §19 that all representations have both an inner and outer dimension, and then in §20, examines in greater detail the representation of our bodies in reference to its inner and outer dimensions. He now considers the inner and outer dimensions of the rest of the field of representations, following his argument that one must conceive of the inner nature of these representations as being analogous to the inner nature of one's body. We do not have a direct access to the inner nature of these representations, so this discussion is done via reflection upon one's body and one's inner nature as will, and a subsequent projection to other representations.

Schopenhauer states that we can distinctly recognize this inner nature as will *per se* in other people, in higher animals, and if we continue to reflect and project the same idea, we can recognize it in the forces that animate plants and that embody physical changes, as in magnetism, and chemical reactions. The inner nature is the same in all, and he refers to this as the "thing-in-itself." It is different in kind from representations and manifests itself as the perceptual field as a whole, that is, as the world.

From the standpoint of the history of philosophy, Schopenhauer's position again closely echoes Berkeley's insofar as the latter similarly recognizes only two fundamental entities, "spirits" and "ideas." These match Schopenhauer's "subjects" and "representations." Relevant to the thoughts in this section, we can mention that Berkeley defines spirit as an active, simple

being that when it produces ideas is called the *will*, foreshadow-
ing Schopenhauer. Moreover, in contrast to spirits, Berkeley
maintains that ideas are passive and inert, and cannot exist in
themselves or without the mind.[20] This reflects how Schopenhauer adopts a significant portion of the Berkeleyan philosophical
framework when he says in this section that Will is *toto genere*
different from the representations it produces.

§22: THE THING-IN-ITSELF AS "WILL"

Attending more closely to our inner nature and our direct
apprehension of it as being of the thing-in-itself, Schopenhauer
now reflects upon his having named it "will." This is noteworthy
with respect to the plausibility or implausibility of the other
candidates for our inner reality that were mentioned above, for
example, cosmic consciousness, time flow, and self-consciousness.
Schopenhauer realizes that within us, our willing is typically
guided by knowledge, as when we make plans and then act
according to the plans. If we are to understand the inner nature
of other beings as well—the animals, for instance—and have a
principle that can effectively explain their appearances and
behaviors, then it is essential to understand the nature of our
willing in a more general way, as being independent of
knowledge.

Schopenhauer accordingly refers to the thing-in-itself as
"Will," but with the precautionary remark that this word should
not be understood in its ordinary sense, as will that is guided
by knowledge, as is the usual case for us. He has in view what
we would refer to in a person or animal as "raw will," or sheer
determination, pure and simple. In this respect, "Will" can
characterize the inner nature of a plant or rock, as well as the
inner nature of a human being or animal. For Schopenhauer,
the difference is only a matter of the degree of complexity.

Against those who might argue that we could use any term to
refer to the thing-in-itself, since what is being referred to is
so vague, Schopenhauer replies that an arbitrary designation
would be appropriate, only if we had no idea what the thing-
in-itself is like. Under such conditions, we should indeed call it
an "X," or unknown entity, as does Kant. To the contrary,
though, Schopenhauer maintains that we have a direct awareness of ourselves as being a fundamentally inner, vital drive, and

so the interpretive and linguistic challenge is to find a word that captures the content of this direct awareness—an awareness that is so close to us, and so immediately felt, that its proximity to us, rather than its distance, renders it difficult to define.

To characterize this direct awareness, Schopenhauer states that it is without form, independent of the principle of sufficient reason, and hence independent of the subject-object distinction. It is consequently timeless and not "known" in the technical sense, where "knowledge" means knowledge of some object. He states that in this kind of special awareness—we can call it philosophical awareness—subject and object coincide. It is a direct, prereflective state of awareness, and one cannot get "behind" it.

§§23–24: THE WORLD APPREHENDED IN TWO WAYS, MECHANICALLY AND WILLFULLY

From what he has now established, Schopenhauer develops two parallel visions of the world. The first is the deterministic vision of the world "as representation"; the second is the thing-in-itself-grounded vision of the world "as will." With respect to the latter, Schopenhauer defines the thing-in-itself in a way partially reminiscent of Kant, for he states that the thing-in-itself is (1) not in space and time (Schopenhauer refers to space and time as the "principle of individuation" [*principium individuationis*]), (2) that it is independent of the subject-object distinction and the principle of sufficient reason as a whole, (3) that it is groundless, and (4) that it is "one." This is the thing-in-itself that manifests itself as the world as representation and which is "Will."

Once Will manifests itself through the principle of sufficient reason, that principle renders Will's appearance mechanical and predictable, even at the level of human behavior. Inanimate objects operate according to the laws of cause and effect, and the same kind of causality operates at the plant and animal levels, only less obviously, but just as surely, in the form of stimulus and response relationships, where a small stimulus could have an unexpectedly powerful response. At the human level, causality fully operates as well, except that it takes the form of behavior according to motives, or "causality that has passed through knowledge."

Human behaviors are difficult to predict, owing to people's capacity for dissemblance, but if it were possible to know a person's character well enough, and understand that person's situation and desires sufficiently, Schopenhauer maintains that the person's behavior would be as predictable as the speed of a falling rock. The world as representation thus conceived of is seamlessly mechanical, deterministic, and fully understandable in principle by scientific, chemical, biological, and psychological investigation. The thoroughgoing scientific knowledge that is implicit, as Schopenhauer emphasizes in Book I, nonetheless provides a metaphysically inadequate and superficial understanding of the world, despite its awesome predictive power.

As a more penetrating and revealing metaphysical vision, Schopenhauer presents an image of the world as the manifestation of the world's underlying will. Once again, human behavior is the most salient case, as we each feel our freedom to act, even as the mechanistic view of nature prescribes how our bodies are determined to move according to the laws of nature. He further points out how animal, plant, and inorganic matter are susceptible to a different, more anthropomorphic characterization—one that reveals the world to be a different place than what the mechanistic view suggests. Our own heartbeat, breathing, digestive processes, sexual impulses, reflex reactions and such, all manifest an inner drive, or will, that the body has to maintain itself, both individually and in view of the species as a whole. Young animals build their shelters, spiders spin their webs, etc., all without knowing why they do so. Their will operates blindly, and yet it wills their behavior effectively for survival. Similarly, one can project a kind of persistence in a magnet's behavior, and in other natural movements and processes. This all forms a picture of the world as the manifestation of Will. Combined with the mechanical vision, we have two sides of the coin.

In §24, Schopenhauer reiterates at some length how mathematical and scientific knowledge provides us with the capacity to know nature thoroughly, but lacks the power to reveal the inner nature of spatio-temporal phenomena. This repeats that no knowledge (in the technical sense of knowledge always being of objects), can penetrate to the inner nature of things, the thing-in-itself. The thing-in-itself is "unknowable," strictly speaking, although this does not prevent us from being directly aware of the thing-in-itself.

Among the many examples of knowledge, he again mentions how we could perfectly predict a person's behavior, if we were to know the person's motives, external circumstances and character. Despite such predictive power, it will remain a mystery to science why the person's character is originally such. This is where scientific explanation fails, and where the thing-in-itself is indicated as a different dimension of things. People's characters appear in the world without explanation, just as do the basic qualities of the chemical elements. We can say that gold or silver has this or that essential property and that it bears such-and-such causal relationships to things, but it remains a mystery why gold and silver exist to begin with.

Schopenhauer believes that these explanatory dead ends indicate that there is another realm of being that is beyond scientific explanation. This is the realm of the thing-in-itself, which without explanation, manifests itself as the scientifically understandable world. The section concludes with a quote from St. Augustine that expresses a more anthropomorphic vision, consistent with Schopenhauer's, where trees desire fertile ground for the sake of bearing more abundant fruit, and where stones, floods, wind, or flame, etc., embody a longing to be what they are, just as a balloon filled with helium expresses a desire to rise in the air. Schopenhauer finds a comrade in Augustine, insofar as the latter's view grasps his idea of "the world as Will."

§25: EVERYONE'S INNER REALITY CONVERGES IN A SINGLE, TIMELESS REALITY

We have seen in §24 how Schopenhauer develops the idea that as it is in itself, the thing-in-itself is wholly different, *toto genere*, from its objectifications, or appearances. Although the thing-in-itself is not in space or time, its objectifications are, and we are governed by the principle of sufficient reason as a whole, of which space and time are aspects. In this section, Schopenhauer continues to explore the distinction between appearance and reality, except that he attends more specifically to how the thing-in-itself is, in itself.

Since plurality emerges only through the principle of sufficient reason, the thing-in-itself is "one," which entails that
literally the same reality underlies each of its manifestations.
The inner reality that one feels in one's body, at its deepest level,
is consequently *identical* with the inner reality that another
person feels within his or her own body, although we normally
do not experience this connection.[21] It is also literally the same
as the inner reality of any particular animal, plant, or rock.
There is only one inner reality and this is the universe's inner
reality. There is only one eye, so to speak, that looks out from the
bodies of people and animals. Since the entire physical world is
the thing-in-itself's objectification, the one eye of the world sees
in an alienated form, only itself.

In such reflections, Schopenhauer is expressing that the world
is a unified whole, that it is essentially a single inner reality, and
that this inner reality presents an objective side to itself. From
observation, he discerns that the world's inner reality, or Will,
presents an objective side that variably reveals its inner nature,
in degrees. Some individuals display Will more intensely than
others, and this yields a series of gradations that range in an
ascending order from inanimate nature, to plants, to animals,
to people.

Appreciating that with respect to oak trees, for instance, it
makes no difference to any particular tree's "oakness," whether
the tree happens to be located in one part of the forest or another,
or living this year, last year, or a decade ago, Schopenhauer
identifies a universal object—in this case, the idea of oakness—
that is Will's "immediate" objectification, in which all individual
oak trees participate and derive their character. The individuals
come and go, but the idea of oakness remains timelessly true.

"Oakness" is just one example among an extensive set of
natural kinds that arrange themselves in a hierarchy and that are
the archetypes of the individuals in the spatio-temporal world.
This field of timeless essences, when set into a spatio-temporal
network, generates multitudes of individuals that express the
respective essences. In a sense, then, every cat that has ever lived
and ever will live, embodies the same universal cat, every person
who has ever lived or will live embodies the same universal
human being, and so on. The multitudes of individuals are mere
appearances. The timeless forms, which Schopenhauer refers to

as Plato's Ideas, are the more fundamental realities. They are universal objects that, when we become aware of them, take us a step closer to the thing-in-itself, that is, to metaphysical truth. Schopenhauer will speak more about our direct apprehension of the Platonic Ideas as grades of the objectification of Will within the context of his aesthetic theory, which we find in Book III.

§26: GRADES OF WILL'S OBJECTIFICATION AND THE INNER NATURE OF NATURAL FORCES

As noted, Schopenhauer believes that all spatio-temporal events admit of a mechanical explanation, and that in such scientific explanations, there comes an inevitable point where natural forces ground the explanation. Schopenhauer mentions gravity and magnetism as examples. It matters not that scientific theories change, for however these forces happen to be defined at the historical time, these elemental forces have no explanation themselves. One can explain the formation of stars by referring to gravitational forces acting on tiny particles, but gravitational force itself is assumed in the explanation. As such, Schopenhauer conceives of these elemental forces as marking the entry points where Will immediately objectifies itself. The forces are instantiated indiscriminately across time and space and are thus conceived of in their essential nature as timeless Platonic Ideas, in terms of which the contingently occurring items in the world of representation receive their structure and content. Since the elemental forces of nature are timeless, there will be no exceptions to the laws of nature within our spatio-temporal experience. The timeless quality of the elemental forces guarantees that all of the instantiations of those forces operate identically.

The natural forces express the lowest grades of Will's objectification, and within this sphere, the various natural objects do not express a high degree of self-expressive individuality. All snowflakes differ, but their differences arise from variable pressures from the external environment. They are all constituted identically by water, and water behaves in the same way under the same conditions, no matter when the conditions occur.

As we ascend the hierarchy of the grades of Will's objectification, the individuals begin to display more intrinsic differences between each other. Earthworms tend to look and behave similarly. Dogs vary dramatically in size and shape across breeds, if we contrast a Chihuahua with a Great Dane, but within a breed, the individual dog's respective personalities form a closer family resemblance. When we come to human beings, the differences between individuals are more noticeable. Each person's character differs from every another, often to the degree that gold differs from silver, and as silver differs from copper. Although all are metals and will behave generally like metals, different metals react in sharply contrasting ways under the same chemical circumstances. They have different melting temperatures, dissolve in different liquids, have different degrees of hardness, and have different chemical weights. The same can hold of two people, for instance, who, when both are put under the same environmental or circumstantial pressures, can act very differently in response.

Schopenhauer also appreciates a timelessness within human intelligible characters that extends beyond any specific historical conditions. Had a particularly honest person who happened to have been born a king or queen, been born as a slave or servant, that person would have acted honestly as a slave or servant. Had a person who happened to have been born as a noninfluential, but violent person, been born in a condition of great privilege and power, that person would still have acted violently. On Schopenhauer's view, when considering a person's intelligible character, it is important to disregard the person's particular historical conditions and to attend exclusive to the quality of that person's inner being, for the historical circumstances are merely the empirical occasion for the expression of the timeless character.

§27: THE STRIVING FOR SELF-PERFECTION AND THE FAILURE OF PHYSICALISTIC REDUCTIONISM

In this lengthy section, Schopenhauer's initial concern is with the legitimacy of the scientific endeavor to reduce, in reference to understanding and explanation, all forms of life to simpler, inorganic forms, that is, to physics. He describes this reductionist program as the attempt to refer the higher grades of Will's objectification to lower grades. Independently of his earlier arguments that scientific explanation always leaves the inner nature of phenomena unexplained, and how it is impossible for objects to cause subjects (a required assumption, if we were to explain consciousness materialistically as brain activity, neurological firings, and such), he now offers some further considerations that cast doubt upon any form of scientific reductionism.

The first consideration is to suggest that reductionism will become less plausible, if we can identify a fundamental format, principle or "type" that is present equally in every grade of Will's objectification, and that is perhaps even more evident in the higher grades. Schopenhauer does not yet identify such a type at this point in his exposition, but notes that the principle of "polarity" comes close, and that throughout the world's philosophies and religions, there has been a perception that polarity permeates the world. His prime example is the Yin-Yang polarity (viz., active-passive; aggressive-tranquil; hard-soft; sharp-diffuse; hot-cold; depending upon the context) that characterizes much Asian religion and thought. He adds that the search for this fundamental type has been a perennial concern, and that the ever-recurring search itself suggests that a single principle underlies all of the world's forms, without giving precedence to any level, to which other levels would be reduced.

Schopenhauer's own version of the fundamental type is the "highly probable" principle of *striving for self-perfection in the midst of perpetual conflict*. This yields a doctrine of emergent properties where at any given level, a set of forces comes into conflict and through that conflict, produces another, new force that summarizes the tendencies of the original conflict, and that perfects those tendencies, also resolving them to some extent. As an example, in a living body there are many chemicals and chemical reactions that are in potential conflict, but these are kept in balance and in mutual support through the body's living, organic quality. Schopenhauer does not believe that this living quality can be explained solely in reference to interacting sets of chemical reactions. Completing the picture, his view is that when the body dies, the conflicts between the forces take over once again, after having lost the balance that life provided. At that point the body begins to decay and as its elements disperse, it soon transforms back into lower grades of Will's objectification.

We should note that Schopenhauer's principle of how more highly developed properties emerge through the resolution of conflict in a striving for self-perfection, is not the principle of dialectical advancement through opposition and resolution, as we find in Hegel, although it bears some similarities to it. Schopenhauer situates his own idea of striving for self-perfection within a sea of perpetual conflict, where complexly organized individuals inevitably return to their earlier and more conflicted conditions, after having had advanced to a more enhanced level. Again, this is evident in the case of living things that inevitably return to an inorganic state after they die.

There is a hierarchy of grades of Will's objectification, ranging from inorganic matter, to plants, to animals, to humans, and although the humans are presently at the top of the hierarchy, human beings do not define or embody the purpose of the world. Humans will disappear at some future time, not necessarily due to the fulfillment of any grand purpose.[22] Schopenhauer's image is of a continual striving, a perpetual effort of one-upmanship on the part of individuals and types, a never-ending contest among natural forms, a repetitive quest for increased power on the part of individuals and their types, a ceaseless struggle, but one that eventually folds its higher members back into the lower ones, only to develop the higher ones again, in a recycling world of eternal recurrence.[23]

Schopenhauer refers to the world's fundamental condition as one of "universal conflict," and since he regards the world of representation as the manifestation of a single Will, this conflict is none other than an inner conflict within Will itself. Will "feasts on itself," as Schopenhauer states, using memorably the image of the bulldog-ant of Australia—an insect that when cut in half, the head attacks the tail, and the tail attacks the head, self-destructively until both halves die. Will's self-feasting is also expressed in the way a moment of time, now present, is effaced by the next moment to time to become present, perpetually. Schopenhauer maintains that the world's perpetual conflict is pointless. It is going nowhere, just as the earth moves through space with no destination.

Schopenhauer observes intriguingly that despite the meaning-less of it all, the striving for self-perfection leads an individual to realize its type well, and that when an individual achieves this, it becomes a beautiful example of its type. *Beauty* thus emerges through conflict, relatively successful striving, self-realization, an increase in strength, and the idea of one's having become (actually) what one (potentially) is. From a physical standpoint, and although the achieved beauty briefly touches what is timeless, such a realization is always short-lived, since it is only a matter of time before the excellently formed individuals disintegrate. For Schopenhauer, though, it remains that the individual rose is no less beautiful because it does not last forever, and this is precisely because the individual reveals the timeless Idea of the rose, which is the genuine object of beauty.

In a reversal of the reductionist program that seeks to understand the higher forms in terms of the lower ones, Schopenhauer describes the hierarchy of Will's gradations by starting with inorganic matter, and then advancing to plants, animals, and humans, observing along the way how the causal relationships typical of inorganic matter give way to the stimuli characteristic of animal life, and how these transform into the motives that move humans intelligently. Within the animal kingdom, Schopenhauer also draws our attention to how knowledge first appears as a means to assist survival, and how it mainly continues along this path in humans. The bulk of our knowledge contributes in one way or another, to growing food, building shelters, constructing defenses, and maintaining the species.

Unique to humans, however, is the capacity to detach our knowledge from our will, and to contemplate things for their own sake, independently of pragmatic, material, survival, or any other worldly concerns. Schopenhauer identifies two spheres where this detachment occurs, the first of which is within art, and the second of which is within saintly resignation. The experience of art prefigures the final goal, which is saintly salvation from the world as representation. Schopenhauer will speak more about these modes of transcendence, in addition to moral awareness, in Books III and IV.

When reading this section's description of the hierarchy of Will's gradations from inorganic, to plant, to animal to human beings, it is tempting to interpret it objectively, as if this hierarchy would occur without the presence of any human beings. This would be too simple of an interpretation, since it is central to Schopenhauer's view that the world as representation appears as a consequence of one's interpreting the thing-in-itself in terms of the principle of sufficient reason. Schopenhauer defines the interpreter in this instance (you, me, etc.) as a timeless subject.

His exposition is thus paradoxical. It begins by stating that from inorganic materials emerge plant and animal life, and from animal life emerge human beings. Once human beings appear, the principle of sufficient reason explicitly comes forth and with it, as he says, the world as representation. The world as representation, considered as a subjective projection of the human being, is the condition for the world as representation, considered as the objective condition for the emergence of the human being, and with it, the world as representation, considered as a subjective projection of the human being.

This is to say that the ascending movement from inorganic nature, to plant and animal life, to humans, implies that my mind, at the point when it historically emerges, is in the perceptual world. As I nonetheless think about everything that appears within my perceptual field, it also follows that that perceptual world is also in my mind. My mind is in my head, which is part of the world as representation, and my head is in my mind. The subject is in the object, and the object is in the subject. We have here, then, the same "strange loop" structure or double containment that we saw earlier in §7. The strange loop informs our situation within the world as representation, which is to say that on Schopenhauer's view, we are in the spatio-temporal world in a philosophically knotted manner, as one might depict by means of a Möbius strip, Klein bottle, or artwork by M. C. Escher, such as *Drawing Hands* (1948).

§28: TIMELESS ACTS OF WILL AND THE WORLD'S VIOLENT APPEARANCE

Schopenhauer provides a broader view of the world in this section, mentioning at first how the various aspects of the world—inorganic, plant, animal, human—are adapted to each other. The soil serves the trees, the trees serve the animals and other plants, the animals and trees serve people, and people act to preserve the environment in many ways. Schopenhauer recognizes this mutual suitability and explains its presence in terms of the oneness of Will that manifests itself as the world as representation. This Will expresses itself in a series of acts, each of which is a universal form expressive of a certain kind of striving. That these diverse acts issue from the same Will, accounts for the world's structural coherence.

In previous sections, Schopenhauer describes these universal forms as Platonic Ideas, as he does here. He now adds that the Platonic Ideas are conceivable as a set of *acts* that stem from the single Will. As acts, the Platonic Ideas are "intelligible characters"; they define a variety of kinds of striving. These include the natural kinds of inorganic matter, the species of plants and animals, and the human beings, where each human is understood to be a unique intelligible character of his or her own, definitive of the individual personality. Schopenhauer adopts the term "intelligible character" from Kant's philosophy, where it refers to human beings' inner character, and expands the notion to include the inner essences of each type of being in the hierarchy of the gradations of Will's objectification.

In terms of discerning the quality of any particular individual's intelligible character, Schopenhauer observes that in inorganic matter, the character is usually presented to us in an immediate and straightforward way, and that as we ascend the hierarchy of gradations of Will, it becomes necessary to observe more of the individual's behavior over time to discern the Idea of which the individual is a manifestation. In human beings, this time can be lengthy, not only because people can dissemble, but because observations of the person in a wide variety of situations might be needed to understand and to test a person's character. How someone acts in peaceful, nonthreatening circumstances might be surprisingly different from how the person acts when mortally threatened.

With respect to explaining the world of representation that we have before us, Schopenhauer reiterates that the hierarchy of the gradations of Will, which are the Platonic Ideas, are arranged timelessly in relation to each other, so what happens within the spatio-temporal realm is not the essential factor. The timelessness of the hierarchy explains why animals build nests, webs, holes, etc., in apparent anticipation of upcoming conditions that it would seem that the animal could not know in advance. Rather than say that the animals have some foresight into the future, one can understand the spatio-temporal world as being governed by timeless relationships between Platonic Ideas. Soil was present spatio-temporally long before oak trees emerged, owing to the timeless relationship between soil and plants. It is not as if the soil ever knew, or ever could know, that the oak trees would be sprouting thousands of years later. Even while it supports the trees, the soil has no idea of what is happening.

Within the spatio-temporal framework, the individuals that instantiate the Platonic Ideas also exhibit tensions between the Ideas as well as harmonies between them, for example, the Idea of a snake conflicts with the Idea of a mongoose. Within the spatio-temporal world, these tensions materialize themselves into a never-ending war where groups of individuals try to exterminate other groups, eternally struggling. Spiders eat flies, cats eat birds, and so on. Given the mutual accord between the Platonic Ideas combined with the mutual tension between them, we have a world that holds together at a fundamental level, but which is filled with violence and suffering. Since the world is a manifestation of Will, and since it is a "hungry," striving Will, each individual—each manifestation of Will—strives at its metaphysical core, and strives to realize the kind of being that it is. The result is constant aggression, exploitation, appropriation, war, and destruction throughout the world as representation.

Schopenhauer maintains that nothing exists besides Will, and that Will is a "hungry" Will. He does not say that nothing exists besides the *thing-in-itself*, and that "Will" is only an aspect of the thing-in-itself, in which case the thing-in-itself might not be thoroughly "hungry," if very hungry at all. The latter possibility would indeed become likely, if the thing-in-itself happened to have an untold number of other aspects, none of which are aptly described with hunger- or desire-related imagery.[24] In this section, Schopenhauer is clear that he believes that the thing-in-itself is wholly "Will," and that nothing else exists besides Will.

§29: WILL: GROUNDLESS, AIMLESS, AND MEANINGLESS

At the beginning of §29, Schopenhauer reiterates the concluding thought from §28 in a summary remark: the world is thoroughly "Will" and thoroughly "representation," and there is nothing beyond this. This confirms that for him, Will is the thing-in-itself proper. When facing the question of what Will is striving or aiming for, Schopenhauer rejects the question by stating that queries of this sort make sense only when we have a situation that allows for motives, and where in view, there is some finite field with an endpoint. In a timeless emptiness, there can be no goal, and if there is a striving, then it must be endless and pointless.[25]

Schopenhauer adds, perhaps more effectively, that reasons make sense only within the sphere of the principle of sufficient reason, and since Will as thing-in-itself is beyond the principle of sufficient reason, there are no reasons for it. The same inability to provide reasons and answers arises when we ask why certain natural forces or elementary particles exist, or why any person has this or that kind of character. Within some given context, we can recite motives and effectively make predictions, but there is no answer to why the person is such to begin with, either as honest, dishonest, courageous, or loyal.

In the world of human experience, Schopenhauer perceives endless flux, recirculation of forms, and no necessary directedness, where every attained end by an individual marks the beginning of another quest, continuing as such up until the point of the individual's demise. Book II thus ends with a vision of teeming masses of individuals that continually feast on each other, all set within a cosmic playing field that stretches infinitely in space and time, with no reason for the constant recirculation of violence and self-destruction. Suffocated by the meaningless suffering inherent in this nightmare, Schopenhauer begins his search for avenues of escape that will provide some peace of mind and final salvation.

STUDY QUESTIONS

1. Why does Schopenhauer believe that mathematics, geometry, the formation of abstract concepts, and all philosophy that grounds itself on the idea of causation, are unable to provide insight into the metaphysical nature of things?

2. What is the significance to Schopenhauer's philosophy of the double-awareness that we have of our bodies?

3. How does the notion of a "strange loop" apply to the structure of Schopenhauer's conception of our place in the world as representation?

4. What role does the notion of a "timeless act" play in Schopenhauer's understanding of (a) why the spatio-temporal

world is filled with violence, and (b) why the spatio-temporal world also retains its basic coherency?

5. Why does Schopenhauer believe that the nature of reality is "Will"?

6. In what sense can we say that Schopenhauer believes that the thing-in-itself is "unknowable"? Does this mean that we cannot have any insight into the nature of the thing-in-itself, as Kant believed?

7. Why does Schopenhauer believe that the world as representation is essentially meaningless?

8. How does Schopenhauer explain the emergence of beauty out of struggle?

9. What is the difference between a person's intelligible character and empirical character, according to Schopenhauer?

SECTION 4. BOOK III, PLATONIC IDEAS, BEAUTY AND ART, §§30–52

§30: REPRESENTATIONS THAT ARE INDEPENDENT OF THE PRINCIPLE OF SUFFICIENT REASON

The subtitle of Book III compares and contrasts with that of Book I, for the latter considers the representation as "subject to" the principle of sufficient reason, whereas Book III now considers it as "independent of" that principle. In its concrete expression, the principle of sufficient reason is a principle relating to finite individuals in space and time, and it defines the form of a person's knowledge, when that person knows some individual object or objects from the standpoint of being an individual subject. Schopenhauer's characterization of the principle of sufficient reason in the present context attends to the notion of individuation, and to avoid confusion, we should recall that he refers to space and time as the *principium individuationis*, that is, the principle of individuation. This *principium individuationis* is at the forefront of his mind here. The above reference in §30's title to the "principle of sufficient reason" is saying, in effect, that Book I considers the representation as it appears in space and time, and that Book III considers the representation as it appears independently of space and time. The latter will involve timeless Platonic Ideas.

The full principle of sufficient reason has a root (the subject-object distinction and the relationship of necessary connection) which has a fourfold expression through (1) abstract concepts, (2) space and time (i.e., geometry and mathematics), (3) causality, and (4) motives. Schopenhauer's titling of Book III gives the impression that he will be examining the representation as it is independent of the principle of sufficient reason in its entirety, but this is misleading. The subject-object distinction remains present throughout Book III, as does a minimalistic notion of differentiation. It would be more precise for him to say that in Book III, he will be considering the representation as it is independently of the fourfold forms of necessary connection as expressed through abstract concepts, geometry and mathematics, causality and motives. Since these constitute the bulk of the principle of sufficient reason, his loose phrasing is understandable.

The representations that are independent of the principle of sufficient reason's fourfold expression are not in time or space (and hence, are not related according to mathematical or geometrical relationships), are not abstract concepts, are not related to each other by relationships of causality, and are not motives for action. They are self-sufficient universal objects, and are the timeless grades of Will's objectification. They are the fixed plans, or archetypes, or "intelligible characters" that define the essences of the individuals that appear in space and time. Although differentiated from each other, these timeless archetypes are each "one" unto themselves, and they suffer no change in quality. They are "objects," but are of a universal, eternal, and timeless sort, as opposed to the less true, perishable individuals that appear in space and time.

Since they are objects, these Platonic Ideas can be "known," but they can be known only under special conditions. The knowing subject must become like them, which is to say that a person must set aside his or her individuality for the sake of adopting a more universalistic perspective, befitting of an ideal human. As it is often characterized, Book III is about Schopenhauer's theory of beauty and art, but it is more fundamentally understood as Schopenhauer's initial inquiry into those situations where people can experience and develop a universalistic perspective and consciousness, and acquire some distance from their more ordinarily desire-filled and suffering-producing individual selves.

§31: SIMILARITIES BETWEEN PLATO AND KANT, AND THE POSSIBILITY OF TRANSCENDING THE UNREALITY OF ORDINARY LIFE THROUGH INTUITION

Schopenhauer describes some similarities between Kant's and Plato's philosophies in §31, observing how they concur that the ordinary world of causally related objects in space and time, is not the true world. From the perspective of the higher reality of which it is a manifestation, this ordinary world is "void and empty," for it is impermanent. The timeless being itself is true, not the individuals that appear in time, for the latter are only the timeless being's perishable manifestations, or objectifications. Plato refers to this timeless being as the realm of Ideas; Kant refers to it as the thing-in-itself.

Within Schopenhauer's metaphysics, the difference between the two aspects of the timeless realm that he recognizes—Will and Platonic Ideas—is slight, and he describes Will as having "immediate objectifications," namely, the Platonic Ideas, all of which are "identical" to Will, except that they are timeless *objects*, whereas Will is not an object.[26] By establishing a virtual identity between Will and the Platonic Ideas, Schopenhauer is able to present his own philosophy as having two main aspects, namely, a timeless, universal aspect and a temporal, individualized aspect. These are specifically, (1) a two-level, timeless aspect constituted by Will as thing-in-itself and the fixed Platonic Ideas, which are Will's immediate objectifications, and (2) a temporal aspect constituted by the perishable objects of our daily experience. These perishable objects are the indirect objectifications of Will, through the lens of the Platonic Ideas.

With respect to our ability to have insight into the timeless dimension, Schopenhauer recognizes that according to Kant, we can have no experience or insight of it and that the thing-in-itself is forever unknowable. Within his own philosophy, however, Schopenhauer maintains to the contrary that we can have an intuitive apprehension of the timeless dimension, as we know from Book II (§18). Book III explores this further. For the most part, Schopenhauer attends to what it is like to apprehend the Platonic Ideas, which constitute the objective side of the timeless dimension. In the concluding section to Book III (§52), he turns to the subjective side of the timeless dimension in the experience of music. This draws our attention again to Will as thing-in-itself, and to the inner nature of things in preparation for Book IV.

§32: THE IDENTITY OF WILL AND THE PLATONIC IDEA

In §32, Schopenhauer considers the distinction between the subjective and objective aspects of the timeless realm by exploring the difference between Will as thing-in-itself and the Platonic Ideas. He formulates his discussion in reference to the difference between Will and "the" Platonic Idea, and to avoid confusion it is important to understand Schopenhauer as reflecting upon the relationship between Will and any given Platonic Idea, rather than to more than one, or even to the whole set of Ideas. For example, since there are obviously many Platonic Ideas (viz., the many gradations of Will that range from inorganic nature, to plants, to animals, to humans), it is easy to become puzzled when encountering Schopenhauer's assertion—and he makes it several times—that there is "no plurality" in the realm of Platonic Ideas.

As noted, Schopenhauer maintains that there is virtually no difference between Will and any particular Platonic Idea. Both are timeless and independent of plurality. The Platonic Idea is a single universal quality that, as Schopenhauer understands it, is internally undifferentiated. The Platonic Ideas of "redness" or "circularity" are clear examples, given the simplicity and uniformity of the Ideas involved.[27] Will and the Platonic Idea are distinguished simply in that unlike Will, the Platonic Idea is an object, or representation, whereas Will is not. The Platonic Idea is the immediate objectification of Will, and Schopenhauer describes this immediacy as introducing only the slightest difference into Will.

Another reason for Schopenhauer's having brought Will and the Platonic Ideas so metaphysically close is to allow that when we apprehend Platonic Ideas, we are coming near to apprehending the nature of things. If aesthetic experience involves the apprehension of Platonic Ideas, as Schopenhauer believes that it does, then the experience of beauty and art will provide metaphysical insight. Artistic geniuses are accordingly conceived of as people who are intuitively connected to the world's timeless dimension.

At one point Schopenhauer states that "pure unclouded knowledge" would arise if, *per impossible*, we were to have *only* Platonic Ideas as the objects of our knowledge. Since we must know things through the medium of our bodies, we can only approximate this purely unclouded condition. Just as he speaks of our apprehension of Will as thing-in-itself through the "thin veil" of time that renders the apprehension slightly imperfect, we can approach this unclouded knowledge of Platonic Ideas, and with it, achieve a sense of being in an "eternal now" (*nunc stans*), where time feels like it is standing still. This is the kind of transcendent awareness that Schopenhauer believes the experience of beauty and art can afford.

§33: KNOWLEDGE AS INITIALLY PRACTICAL AND SURVIVAL-RELATED

Schopenhauer reminds us that knowledge, in the strict sense, is governed by the principle of sufficient reason and that as humans, we grew physically out of the natural sequence of being that begins with inorganic matter, and then advances to the plant and animal kingdoms. As we stand as a living upshot of this sequence—a sequence which is itself a manifestation of Will—we emerged with the survival-valuable capacities of reflection, abstraction, and logic. From this standpoint, human knowledge is *prima facie* practically geared, and focused mainly on spatio-temporal objects. It is fundamentally in the service of Will.

Schopenhauer notes that an apprehension of timeless objects is nonetheless possible, and that this requires a sharp change in the subject's orientation, for a timeless object requires for its access, a timelessly oriented subject. To apprehend Platonic Ideas, it is consequently necessary to disengage from practical interests, from looking forward into the future, and from one's sense of being an individual, desire-filled, egoistic being.

§§34–35: THE "WORLD AS REPRESENTATION" AS A TIMELESS PANORAMA OF PLATONIC IDEAS

To apprehend an ordinary object's Platonic idea, one must further devote one's attention to the object's immediate perceptual presence, such as to "lose oneself" in that object. The aim is to consider only the "what," or perceptual qualities of the object that reveal the kind of thing it is, and disregard where the object is, when it is, and where it came from. One ignores the object's spatio-temporal and causal dimensions insofar as these are extraneous to the object's immediate perceptual presentation.

This aesthetic attitude matches generally how one apprehends oneself as "Will" through a "thin veil" that excludes space and causality, and includes time only insofar as aesthetic experiences are felt to take place in an "eternal now." The difference is that in aesthetic perception, with which we are now dealing, we focus outward toward some physical object as an object *per se*, as opposed to trying to feel that object's inner being, as we might feel the inside of our hand. Using our hand as an example, in the first instance we feel the inside of our hand and apprehend Will as thing-in-itself, as Schopenhauer describes in Book II. In the aesthetic mode of apprehension, now before us in Book III, we apprehend shining through our hand, the Platonic Idea that resides behind and within all hands, and thus apprehend our own hand—which could just as well be anyone else's hand that we are perceiving—as the timeless hand, as the same hand that is part of every other human and handed animal. We are thus not losing ourselves in the mere richness and extensiveness of the immediate perceptual details, as one would have in a purely aestheticist mode of consciousness, but are penetrating insightfully through all those details to apprehend the object's pure and timeless kind.

Schopenhauer's view is that when we adopt this kind of aesthetic attitude, the timeless quality of the perceived object shows itself, and the object assumes an ideal quality that conveys the reality of every object of its kind, independently of when or where it might exist. When we aesthetically contemplate a tree, we regard the tree as not this particular tree, but as the timeless Tree. The tree's ideal form shines through the individual details strongly, and one apprehends the ideal form almost exclusively. One sees a person on the street, and appreciates shining through that person, virtually *as* that person, humanity itself; one sees a tulip in the flower shop, and sees shining through that tulip, the being of every tulip that has ever been and will be. If we were to focus such an aesthetic attention upon our body as a whole, in conjunction with our behaviors, we would be in the position to discern our own intelligible characters and acquire self-knowledge.

Since we disregard the past and future and attend to the present within this kind of aesthetic awareness, there are no significant projections into the future that could be associated with desires, their frustrations, and their satisfactions. One becomes "will-less" in this sense, and the bulk of the suffering associated with unfulfilled desires dissolves. One becomes purified of desire and in Schopenhauer's wording, becomes a "pure" subject of knowing. Minimizing one's desires amounts to a kind of self-purification, and upon assuming such a purifying attitude, one's feelings of "Kantian" time, that is, past-present-future-oriented time, also dissolve to generate the feeling that time is standing still, or that one is in an "eternal present."

Schopenhauer describes this aesthetic mode of awareness in idealized terms, saying that the pure subject of knowledge is *wholly* will-less, painless, timeless, universal, and nonpersonal. He contrasts this with the "knowing individual" who is filled with desire, projections into the future, discernments of cause and effect relationships, rationalizations, concerns with merely spatio-temporal objects, and hence, suffering. Since Schopenhauer acknowledges that we must always experience ourselves and the world through our bodies (§18), his characterizations of the knowing individual versus the pure subject of knowledge are best regarded as theoretical extremes that in actual life are always combined and tempered to some degree. It remains that we can closely approximate the timeless feeling that Schopenhauer associates with the perception of Platonic Ideas, acknowledge that these Ideas can be perceived, and admit that the outlook is notably different from that of being pragmatically engaged in the quest for satisfying one's more mundane desires in the spatio-temporal world.

The latter part of §34 can easily generate some bewilderment upon reading that the aesthetic attitude generates a *complete* objectification of Will, and that this allows us to apprehend the "true" world as representation. The potential confusion issues from how throughout most of the section, Schopenhauer attends to the perception of some single object, and how the perception of this object can lead to the apprehension of the object's

Platonic Idea. One then wonders how the *entire* world as representation can suddenly enter into the discussion, when Schopenhauer has only been describing the experience of, say, aesthetically contemplating a tree or a rock.

In the exposition, there is an unannounced jump from Schopenhauer's description of the aesthetic contemplation of a single object, to the related idea of opening one's eyes to the world as a whole to survey it with this aesthetic attitude. At the end of the section, Schopenhauer explains that he has been describing what it is like for someone to aesthetically appreciate nature *as a whole*, and how, upon doing this, the person realizes as a universal consciousness, that the world is being supported by that very consciousness.

When we survey nature as a whole with this aesthetic attitude, Schopenhauer's thought is that we will apprehend, almost exclusively, the Platonic Ideas that correspond to the perceptual items in view, and if we are presumably perceiving examples of inorganic nature, plants, animals, and humans, as when walking through a park filled with people enjoying picnics and such, we will consequently apprehend a representative set of Platonic Ideas and hence, the "true" world as representation. This is the timeless version of the world as an "object" that is closest to Will itself. To the extent that we lose ourselves in the objects that are being contemplated, and insofar as the objects contemplated are now Platonic Ideas, we become the timeless subjective correlate of the Ideas, and hence, approach being aware of ourselves as the very Will as thing-in-itself that immediately objectifies those Ideas. From this follows Schopenhauer's thought of how, at this juncture, we become aware of ourselves as the supporters of the world, along with his motivations for quoting from the *Upanishads* at the end.

Section 34 presents one of the key experiences that generates Schopenhauer's vision of the world, for his own aesthetic experience of things contributes significantly to his philosophical vision. To understand his philosophy, it helps considerably to adopt an aesthetic attitude toward the spatio-temporal world as a whole, as he understands that attitude.

Apprehending the Platonic Ideas of ordinary objects is a meaning-filled experience, for as he describes in §35, we soon come to appreciate the array of atmospheric forces that move the clouds, the gravitational forces that pull the rivers across the soil and stones, not to mention the continual emergence and passing away of individual human beings, where the basic characters and types of narratives continually recur. Schopenhauer mentions that within such an aesthetic panorama, a person might initially lament how, within the field of historical accident, tremendous opportunities have been lost, as people who could have enriched human culture were killed by chance, or were distracted from realizing their potential. He adds consolingly that such lamentation would be unfounded, for the fundamental reality is the set of Platonic Ideas that instantiate themselves without gain or loss, inexhaustibly. There are no lost treasures in the end: what did not happen within this particular historical epoch, will happen in another; what was unrealized in one instance will be realized in another. The individuals involved will not matter as such, nor will the time and place of the realization, since the truer reality is timeless. The instantiations are merely transitory.

We can pause to notice that Schopenhauer has not yet referred to art or beauty, but has been interested more generally in the time-stilling experience of Platonic Ideas, insofar as the experience is metaphysically revelatory and is "pure," "will-less," and "painless." His primary interest is in the apprehension of Platonic Ideas, not their apprehension necessarily through art or in reference to beauty *per se*, although art and beauty figure into his discussion. From Book II (§27) we can recall that Schopenhauer defines beauty as the apprehension of ideal types, for example, of the timeless form that can be apprehended through "perfect specimens," in the plant and animal context. He now considers "art" as a way to apprehend these types.

§§36–37: THE ENHANCED PRESENTATION OF PLATONIC IDEAS THROUGH ART, AS ENVISIONED BY THE ARTISTIC GENIUS

Plato's Allegory of the Cave, which Schopenhauer now mentions in §36, inspires his aesthetics in general, and in particular, his understanding of aesthetic perception, artistic genius, and the nature of art. The Allegory appears in the *Republic* (Book VII), where Plato presents the image of a set of prisoners in a subterranean cavern, immobilized with chains and facing a large wall, who are in the position only to watch shadowy movements upon the wall as if it were a large movie screen. The wall contains the shadows cast by the movements of people who, unbeknownst to the prisoners, walk behind the prisoners on a parapet and who carry various everyday objects in front of a large fire. The prisoners perceive only the shadow world on the wall, and are thoroughly accustomed to watching the shadows, predicting the shadows' movements, and commending each other for their respective skills in predicting those movements.

At one point, one of the prisoners becomes free of his chains, escapes from the cavern, and ascends into the brightly lighted area above ground. After his eyes become accustomed to the new environment, he apprehends the real objects of the ordinary world, along with the illuminating sun. Returning later to the cavern, the prisoner benevolently attempts to share his knowledge of the higher reality that resides at the basis of the cavern's shadow world, but as the community of prisoners observes that he is unable to see well in the dark, let alone in the light, presumably, the community fails to take him seriously. They soon regard the persistent prisoner as mad and as a threat to their social practices. In due time, they threaten his life for continuing to speak so absurdly.

In Schopenhauerian and Platonic terms, the prisoners' shadow world is the scientifically understandable world of space, time, and causality. It corresponds to our so-called real world with it suns and galaxies. The prisoners' shadow world corresponds to the realm of the concrete, fourfold expression of the principle of sufficient reason, which includes among its modes of understanding, the disciplines of physics, mathematics, geometry, psychology, and the remaining sciences. This is the realm of individual objects and of abstract concepts drawn from perception. According to Schopenhauer, it is an illusory world.

The prisoner who becomes free to behold the sunlight—in Plato, this is the philosopher who acquires true knowledge—is the one who, by analogy, can apprehend the Platonic Ideas, who can transcend his or her spatio-temporal condition, and who can put himself or herself into a condition of timeless, desire-free perception. In Schopenhauer's rendition, this person is the artistic genius, who naturally has a capacity to apprehend any object and discern through it, the ideal type, or Platonic Idea, that shines through it.

In his allegory, Plato reflects briefly on how a person who has been dwelling in the daylight for an extended period might appear to those who remain in the dark, and who have known only that benighted world. As noted, the person could very well appear to be mad, and in §36, Schopenhauer considers some of the coincidences between genius and madness, which, despite their important differences, stem from how both geniuses and mad people allegedly disregard the past and maintain an exclusive attention to the present moment. As Schopenhauer observes, they nonetheless do so for different reasons: the genius ignores the past on account of his or her exclusive attention to a timeless form; the mad person appears to suppress the awareness of the past in order to keep tormenting memories away.[28] The genius may present a semblance of madness to those who live in the shadows of the principle of sufficient reason, but the genius is not mad.

Although Plato's Allegory of the Cave inspires Schopenhauer's aesthetics and philosophy, we should note that Plato's own views of art are diametrically opposed to Schopenhauer's. Plato unsympathetically regards artists as copiers of the items in the spatio-temporal world, and as people who lead us further into ignorance. Plato regards the artistic copies of the items of the ordinary world as the shadows of shadows, and this locates them at a metaphysical distance twice removed from the timeless truths. Contrary to Plato, Schopenhauer appreciates how works of art can idealize and perfect the forms of daily life and present Platonic Ideas more directly and clearly than ordinary objects. In opposition to science and the principle of sufficient reason, Schopenhauer regards art as a superior form of knowledge, for the objects it reveals are those that serve as the fixed archetypes of our fluctuating daily world.

The artistic genius is someone who, more naturally than most people, can become a pure subject of knowing that grasps the ideal qualities of things. The genius's visions are then embodied in works of art, whose function is to reveal the visions of timeless realities to others. Schopenhauer is not concerned with either natural beauty or artistic beauty *per se*, and he does not emphasize strongly or preferably how the apprehension of

the Platonic Ideas arises for this or that person. He attends
exclusively to the perception of Platonic Ideas, and speaks indiscriminately of a tree that is a perfect specimen and a good
painting of tree, if both stimulate the apprehension of Platonic
Ideas to the same degree.

§38: WILLING, FRUSTRATION, DISINTERESTED PERCEPTION, AND PEACE

Schopenhauer recalls that the subject-object distinction can
be instantiated at one of two levels: the subject and object can
appear either as individual beings, or they can appear as universal beings. In the former, an individual person knows individual
objects, and in the latter, a universal subject—a "pure, will-less
subject of knowledge"—knows universal objects, or Platonic
Ideas. The universal subject-object distinction corresponds to
the general root of the principle of sufficient reason; the individual subject-object distinction corresponds to the principle's
fourfold expressions that bear on space, time, causality, desire,
mathematics, geometry, and science. Although Schopenhauer
speaks of "abandoning" the principle of sufficient reason to
ascend to the universal mode of knowing, this is actually a call
to shed the principle's fourfold modes of expression for the
sake of ascending to a condition defined more generally by the
most universal way of knowing.

Section 38 contains one of Schopenhauer's most often-quoted
passages that describes our ordinary state of being, which is
being filled by willing. On his view, willing is the expression of a
lack or need. It is the feeling of something missing, and of being
pulled toward some promising object. Schopenhauer is certain
that after acquiring the object of our desire, our satisfaction will
fade, and new feelings of desire and hunger will rise up again to
take the place of the former ones. Although at any given moment
it perpetually seems as if acquiring the new objects of desire
will help us to become permanently satiated, content, and happy,
the sad fact is that our desires only drive us on for more.

One might react disbelievingly to Schopenhauer's claim that
desire is painful, observing that when we look forward to pleasurable times (say, a long-awaited vacation) we certainly "lack"
those times at present, but rather than suffer, we experience a

kind of satisfaction. In reply, it can be said that the perceived satisfaction arises from partially satisfying our desire with the image of the future pleasures. The pleasure arises from satisfying the desire in imagination, and by setting aside the conflicting thought that the desire has not actually been satisfied. If one were to discover that the anticipated vacation must be cancelled, then the reality of the original lack involved would immediately show itself, and one would experience the pain and frustration that Schopenhauer indicates is at the bottom of all desire. When we do not fill the gap with imaginary substitutes that produce a dreamlike satisfaction, desires are painful when we realize that the objects of desire are not in fact present.

Taking seriously the idea that after being satiated, the satisfaction soon fades, only to issue in new desires, Schopenhauer realizes that this natural condition conflicts with being calm, tranquil, and peaceful. The human condition is thus expressed well by classical Greek personages of eternal frustration, such as Ixion, who, pinned to a flaming wheel, was suspended in a condition of inescapably burning pain. It is also reflected in the Danaids, who were condemned to scoop water into vessels using useless strainers. Tantalus also personifies it in his condition of eternal hunger: desperately in need of food, but held in bondage, Tantalus stretches his head toward some fruits that hang tantalizingly near, only to watch the objects of his desire draw away from him to remain a hair's breath beyond his reach. Schopenhauer invokes these images to reveal the nature of ordinary life, which he regards as a prison governed by instinctual and petty desires, and which we experience as a predominantly painful, frustrating, and disappointing environment.

In a quest for peace, painlessness, freedom, and relief, Schopenhauer notes that of all the creatures on earth, only humans have the capacity to self-consciously diminish the effectiveness of their instinctual drives. This gives us the power to experience a transcendent state of awareness by immersing ourselves in perception, losing ourselves in the objects perceived, and rising insightfully through them to an apprehension of timeless archetypes. The aesthetic experience can occur anywhere in principle, with any object, and Schopenhauer praises the Dutch still-life painters for showing us how the most mundane and insignificant objects can lift us out of the field of natural desire to a blessed, more tranquil, will-free frame of mind.

Some sense-modalities are more effective than others in lifting us out of mundane, desire-filled existence. Smell and taste are the least effective, since we tend to be viscerally affected strongly and immediately by them. Touch is also sensuous and desire-centered, although we can sometimes savor the texture of objects for their own sakes. Sounds also remain close to the will, but they sometimes offer the opportunity to experience purity in perception. The optimal sense modality is the sense of sight, for we can savor the reflections of objects in water, or appreciate abstract designs, without any will to own or consume the objects. Such experiences are delightfully detached, and most conducive for experiencing knowledge through pure perception, where we lose our sense of physical individuality.

§39: THE "STRANGE LOOP" OF THE SUBLIME

Having noted in §38 how different sense-modalities can either reinforce or interfere with our efforts to assume the perspective of a pure, painless, will-less subject of knowing in aesthetic perception, Schopenhauer attends to some of these impediments more explicitly, addressing how the fear of bodily harm, intensely lustful or sensuously captivating attraction and strong visceral repulsion can affect, and even preclude our efforts to achieve a disinterested, universalistic state of aesthetic contemplation. These are Schopenhauer's discussions of the sublime, the disgusting, and the charming.[29]

According to Schopenhauer, the experience of the sublime occurs when the perceptual object that we aim aesthetically to contemplate, initially overwhelms us, either because it threatens to harm us, or because it is too large to encompass in a single imaginative sweep. Since there are degrees of feeling threatened or feeling overwhelmed in size, there are different intensities of the sublime, all of which have as their purpose the perception of Platonic Ideas and the experience of beauty. Schopenhauer regards the sublime as a variety of beauty, rather than as a separate aesthetic category of its own.

Objects that stimulate the experience of sublime can range from a quiet, peaceful, but stark and environmentally sparse desert, to tremendous storms, blasting and crashing with thunder and lightning at every turn. Schopenhauer's discussion presents a spectrum of threatening and large objects that stimulate the experience of the sublime in a variety of corresponding intensities. To grasp the essence of the matter, let us consider the sublime in its most characteristic form.

The full effect of the sublime consists of two phases. First, there is a feeling of being "reduced to nothing," either by perceiving how our bodies are reduced imaginatively to a mere speck through a contrast with the infinite extent of space and time, or by sensing the approach of our body's annihilation by overwhelmingly powerful physical forces. In both cases, we perceive ourselves as objects, and eventually as insignificant beings within the world of representation, one among billions, and as virtually nothing in the vast scheme of things. The second phase of the sublime experience involves a reversal in perspective as we turn away from the worries and frustrations related to the will, and recognize ourselves as beings—as knowing subjects— within which the very mental images of our threatened bodies, space, and time, are themselves contained.

In its elementary form, the experience of the sublime involves the initial awareness that one's mind, or consciousness, is located in one's small, fragile, and transient body, which is itself situated in an extensive and turbulent physical universe. However, this initial awareness then transforms into the realization that one's body is in one's mind, that is, that the body is only a set of mental images within one's consciousness, and that it is one's mind itself that contains as a set of mental images, or representations, that very physical universe, which includes the forms of space and time. As we have seen in earlier sections (§7 in Book I and §27 in Book II), this "double-containment" or "strange loop" structure that displays the twofold nature of consciousness, is one of the fundamental structures within Schopenhauer's philosophy. It emerges once again here in Book III, in Schopenhauer's account of the sublime.

§40: THE CHARMING, THE DISGUSTING, AND THE PORNOGRAPHIC

Schopenhauer defines beauty as the experience of a spatio-temporal object through which shines that object's ideal type, or

Platonic Idea, where in the contemplation of that Idea, we forget ourselves as individuals and enjoy a relatively will-free, disengaged, peaceful state of mind. Unlike the experience of the sublime, and as is common knowledge, some art depicts objects that engage our wills in a less aesthetically productive way. For instance, we can be attracted by portrayals of luscious food or of seductive bodies that promise sexual satisfaction, or we can be repulsed by portrayals of bodily liquids such as mucus or pus. In general, the portrayal of sex and death in art tends to captivate our wills, and this conflicts with Schopenhauer's conception of ideal aesthetic experience.

Schopenhauer believes that the best art—at least for most people—would avoid or minimize such desire-increasing subject matters, since the way their images and themes drive a person to have a more intense awareness of himself or herself as an individual bodily presence in space and time, tends to undermine the attitude of detachment required for aesthetic contemplation. Rather than raising us to a more desire-free level of consciousness, such works support a desire-filled mentality and entrench us more solidly in the world of the fourfold expression of the principle of sufficient reason. Within a Schopenhauerian framework, such artworks only generate more suffering, as when one throws gasoline upon a fire.

Pornographic imagery is among the most straightforward cases of this phenomenon, since it is designed specifically to stimulate and increase the intensity of one's desire. When it does so through the presentation of beautiful, idealized human bodies, the display of ideal types becomes infused with intense desire, producing in Schopenhauerian terms, a metaphysically contradictory mixture. In such cases, imagery that would otherwise stimulate a contemplative detachment from life, as we find in classical Greek sculpture, combines with a sexually oriented presentation that stimulates the strongest affirmation of life. Stendhal's remark that "La beauté n'est que la *promesse* du bonheur" (beauty is nothing but the *promise* of happiness) is instructive to reflect upon in this context, since to the contrary, Schopenhauer would regard the charming beauty that pornographic imagery often contains, as a promise of frustration and boredom, once the sexual stimulation is allowed to take effect.[30]

Schopenhauer conceives of charming and disgusting subject matters as the true opposite of the sublime, presumably because people do not usually transcend the subjects portrayed, but become wrapped up in them to become more intensely filled with desire or repulsion. There are nonetheless some affinities to the experience of the sublime that Schopenhauer does not develop, and these emerge once we draw the distinction between an object (such as a luscious plate of food, attractive physical body, actual blood, etc.) and the representation of that object.

Aristotle observed in his *Poetics* that as opposed to the real thing, the representations of highly disturbing (or highly attractive) episodes or objects, such as violence and death, allow us to apprehend the objects with less emotional attachment.[31] The representations provide the opportunity to learn more about and understand the objects with a measure of detachment and release from their ordinarily fear-generating or lust-generating effects. In this more distanced respect, the artistic portrayal of a luscious plate of food or a sexually attractive body can be instructive and can support a properly aesthetic attitude toward the object. When we confuse the representation with the real thing and apprehend the representation as a virtual reality, taking the image of the food for actual food, or the pornographic image of a sexually attractive body for an actual body, there is a greater danger of gravitating into the will-suffused situation of which Schopenhauer is so critical.

Schopenhauer does recognize a more aesthetically oriented attitude toward will-stimulating representations at the end of §39 in his characterization of the sublime character. This is displayed by someone who can observe other people and things in an objective way, independent of the relations those people and things might have to his or her will. Such a character will observe people who project despising attitudes, without feeling anger, hate, or aggression toward the offending individuals. A person with a sublime character will similarly be able to appreciate others' good luck and happiness without feeling envy, and will be able to perceive sexually attractive bodies without feeling any lust, and so on.

One would presume, then, that a person with a sublime character will be able to appreciate art that contains a solid measure of charming or disgusting subject matter. When Schopenhauer

advises that such subjects be avoided in art, he speaks in reference to the likely and common reactions, rather than to the rare
sublime reaction to such artistic presentations. The charming
and disgusting subject matters, one might say, are aesthetically
suitable only for metaphysically enlightened audiences.

§§41–42: DIMENSIONS OF BEAUTY AND THE HIERARCHY OF PLATONIC IDEAS

Schopenhauer considers two dimensions of beauty in §41 that
define beauty's intensity. The first concerns how readily an object
facilitates aesthetic contemplation. Snowflakes and flowers, for
instance, when they are well-formed, virtually invite us to contemplate them aesthetically, whereas well-formed flies or bees
are less immediately attractive, as fascinating as their forms may
become once we attend to them disinterestedly. Snowflakes and
flowers are thus more beautiful along this dimension, than flies
and bees.

The second dimension of beauty concerns the respective
contents of the Platonic Ideas contemplated. There is an ascending hierarchy of Ideas, ranging from those of inorganic nature to
those of human beings, and the higher we ascend, the richer the
Ideas become. Schopenhauer consequently asserts that human
beings are the most beautiful in reference to their meanings, and
that the highest aim of art is to express human qualities. Each
art can be appreciated furthermore in reference to its capacity to
express this or that dimension of human meaning, for example,
plastic arts center upon human form and expressiveness, literary
arts are effective for presenting human conduct, and music is
best for embodying human feeling.

Depending upon the level of the Idea contemplated, the
aesthetic pleasure will center respectively more upon the subject
or upon the object. The Ideas of inorganic nature—and
Schopenhauer has in mind here only natural kinds, rather than
artificially constructed items—have only a thin content, and so
the aesthetic pleasure resides mainly in the subject's tranquillity
that contemplating such Ideas can afford. Once we ascend into
Ideas relative to the higher animals and especially to humans,
the richer content of the Ideas more significantly contributes to
the aesthetic pleasure.

§§43–44: THE BEAUTY OF INORGANIC, PLANT, AND ANIMAL ARCHETYPES IN ART

Considered as an art, Schopenhauer maintains that architecture's purpose is to display the lower-level Platonic Ideas of natural forces in a clear way. Gravity pulls constructions downward; rigidity holds them up. The structure of a building may be complicated in terms of how it distributes these forces, but Schopenhauer believes that our contemplation of the basic forces of gravity and rigidity, as expressed by the architectural work, is at the crux of the aesthetic experience of architecture.

Ideally, every part of a building should be arranged to have each part depend upon every other, to display effectively the array of physical tensions that the building embodies. The building should be constructed as an organic unity. The materials should be presented so that the perceiver can have an accurate perception of the forces that are at work. The stronger the forces displayed, also the better, so Schopenhauer frowns on buildings made of wood or lighter materials. He also discourages deceptive presentations where the building appears to be made of heavy materials, but is actually constructed out of lighter ones.

In addition to inorganic forces such as gravity, rigidity, cohesion, and hardness, the presence of light is also integral to the aesthetic perception of architecture. The play of reflections, shadows, and brightly illuminated areas reveal the contours and forces within the building, as they also reveal the nature of light itself. In this respect, architecture involves the aesthetic appreciation of light as well as of elementary physical forces. The same kind of appreciation that is relevant to architecture, also obtains in connection with artificially constructed fountains, waterfalls, and rivulets. Inorganic forces similarly operate here, except that instead of gravity standing in conflict with rigidity, gravity pulls water downward to allow it to move pleasingly and freely.

Section 44 takes us to the next level in the hierarchy of Platonic Ideas to consider the apprehension of plant and animal Ideas through art. Formal gardens present the Ideas of plants, but the gardens themselves do not endure long in any one particular condition. Their forms also tend to be unruly, owing precisely to the living nature of the plants that constitute them. For a better apprehension of the plant Ideas, landscape painting offers a sharper idealization and a more permanent presentation.

Animal painting and sculpture share the same kind of aesthetic advantage over actual animals, and in reference to this subject matter, we also advance to a level of aesthetic apprehension where the content of the Idea presented becomes more intriguing. We consequently take careful notice of the animals' posture and expression, as we aim to apprehend the quality of their inner being.

Having now moved from the Ideas of inorganic nature, to those of plants and animals, virtually the entire spectrum of Platonic Ideas has been covered in terms of its main representatives, so if we were aesthetically to contemplate a garden containing some animals (e.g., birds, squirrels, etc.), we would be able to apprehend a sample of the spectrum of the hierarchy of Platonic Ideas that underlies the world. This would generate an experience of the panorama of Platonic Ideas similar to what Schopenhauer describes in §§34–35 above. He adds here that we can also perceive the oneness of Will beneath those Ideas and experience of universal identity of subject and object described by the Upanishadic words, *tat tvam asi* (that is *you*).[32]

§§45–47: THE IDEALLY BEAUTIFUL HUMAN FORM IN SCULPTURE

Schopenhauer begins in these sections to attend to the artistic expression of the highest Idea, namely, the Idea of humanity. This Idea expresses a generic conception that disregards the specific character of each individual, akin to how as a rule, classical Greek sculpture displays generically formed human bodies, but not specific individuals, as emerge later in Roman sculpture. Recognizing, however, that each person's character is a unique Platonic Idea of its own, Schopenhauer tries to locate a balance between the beauty of humanity, which expresses the generic human conception, and the personal qualities of any given individual, which are not constitutive of human beauty at the general level, strictly speaking.

Observing realistically that few people, if any, exactly embody the ideally beautiful human form, Schopenhauer asks how the artist can formulate this Idea in his or her art, especially in connection with sculptural expression. His answer is that the artistic process is not mechanical, and that it involves vision and insight into what is characteristic in a person. He adds that the artist needs to include *grace* as part of the ideal presentation, for although purely static forms can be beautiful, a complete Ideal image of a beautiful person requires a temporal dimension as well. This is achieved by adding some grace, which lends the feeling of pleasantly composed, smooth, and poised movement, like that of a dancer.

Schopenhauer observes in connection with the famous *Laocoön* group, which depicts a man (a priest of Troy) and his two sons under attack by serpents, that the priest's mouth is open, but owing to the silent nature of stone sculpture, there is, of course, no shriek to be heard. Reacting to an array of scholarly discussions of the work, Schopenhauer argues that if the artwork is to be interpreted as being consistent with the nature of sculpture itself, then we should conclude that no shriek is even being represented, contrary to other accounts. His point is to show that art criticism needs to remain aware of the respective parameters of the various art media in question, and to circumscribe its critical observations to what is possible within the media. It would be out of bounds to criticize the television presentation of a gourmet chef, for instance, because the presentation does not supply the appropriate odors and felt textures of the food.

Insofar as sculpture intends to represent the ideal human form, Schopenhauer also advises that drapery in sculpture should function to reveal the contours of the human body. As opposed to using thick, heavy, or highly decorated clothing that obscures bodily expression, the drapery should be thin and tasteful, to convey a natural and relaxed bodily pose.

§§48–50: ACADEMIC PAINTING, IDEAL PAINTING, AND IMPURE PAINTING

Academic painting traditionally recognizes a hierarchy of painting types, or genres, valued according to their subject matter. At the lowest levels are landscapes, still lifes, and animal paintings, since the objects portrayed are nonhuman. At the middle levels are portraits and genre paintings, which show scenes from daily human life. At the upper levels are paintings of historical, religious, mythological, and literary subjects, since these portray human beings, and sometime gods, engaged in significant social activity.

Schopenhauer does not strongly object to this hierarchical organization, but he observes that it does not capture the purpose of painting well, which is to reveal the many-sided and timeless quality of the Idea of humanity. To achieve this, one need not show people acting in a major historical event, since first of all, some historical events are superficial in spiritual content, and second, since the universal qualities sought are usually independent of such events.

The *inner character* of humanity is most important to portray, and this involves revealing the diversity and timelessness of human character, where the substance of the characters themselves is independent of historical or religious circumstances. Schopenhauer mentions, for example, that with regard to the inward significance of the characters and actions involved, it might be exactly the same, whether we refer to government officials who compete over the control of countries drawn on map, or whether we refer to ordinary people in a beer-house clashing over cards and dice, as we might find in a genre painting. The kinds of people, psychological attitudes and such, might be essentially the same.

Crucial to painting, then, is not that some significant historical event is portrayed, but that some timeless truth or depth of character regarding the human being is revealed. This can be achieved in genre painting, in portraits, in historical or in religious painting. Conversely, no particular kind of painting implies of itself that the painting will be of great human significance. Some religious, some historical, some portraits, some genre paintings are of trivial or empty subjects, and do not realize painting's main task.

As examples of the highest achievements of painting, Schopenhauer does not in fact refer us to historical works, but cites generically composed portraits of religious figures, as exemplified in the works of Raphael and Correggio. Of interest to him is not the works' religious affiliation, but the facial expressions, which reveal a peaceful composure consistent with how someone might look, if the person had had the Schopenhauerian vision of apprehending the hierarchy of Platonic Ideas, and of consequently seeing through the individualities and contingencies of the spatio-temporal world.

At the summit of visual art for Schopenhauer, are paintings that present such peacefully knowing figures—one can include images of Buddha here—and that convey a feeling of detachment from all willing. The artworks bring time to a standstill for the perceiver, and move the perceiver to point where resignation and salvation from the spatio-temporal world becomes a seriously contemplated possibility.

Schopenhauer reiterates in §49 that the apprehension of Platonic Ideas is not a common capacity, adding that the finest works of art will not be perceived or appreciated as such by the bulk of humanity. It is more common to encounter works constructed mechanically and formulaically according to abstract concepts, where their being depends upon lifeless rules and procedures. For Schopenhauer, these works do not live up to what art ought to be, and he does not regard them as true art. Unlike abstract concepts, which are fixed summaries of already experienced items, the true foundation of art resides in the Platonic Ideas, which are the original plans of the very perceptual items from which abstract concepts are later extracted.

To appreciate Schopenhauer's repeated criticism of abstract concepts, we can compare his conception of abstract concepts to Plato's negative conception of art, mentioned above in the discussion of §§36–37. According to Plato, ordinary perceptual objects are imperfect, spatio-temporal copies of the truer, perfect, and timeless Platonic Ideas. Schopenhauer agrees with Plato on this point. According to Plato, however, works of art are nothing more than copies of these imperfect perceptual objects, as a two-dimensional drawing of a fish copies a real, three-dimensional one, and is that much further removed from the Idea of the fish. Schopenhauer disagrees with this Platonic conception of art, but his own negative conception of *abstract concepts* compares almost exactly to Plato's negative conception of artistic representations. We can say of both that they (1) are twice removed from the core reality of Platonic Ideas, (2) are the fainter, and more lifeless copies, and (3) are the last items we should be looking at, if we are to apprehend the truth, since ordinary perceptual objects are metaphysically closer to the Platonic Ideas than are the shadows of those perceptual objects.

Painting or sculpture that substantially incorporates content from abstract concepts thus receives a disapproving evaluation from Schopenhauer. His main example is when the paintings or sculptures have allegorical or symbolical content, that is, when the work signifies something different from what it depicts. A rose could be meant to signify secrecy, blue could be meant to signify fidelity, and so on. These are like a candelabrum whose base is a sculpture, or a warrior's shield that contains an elaborate bas-relief that might be destroyed during a battle, or worse yet, a beautiful candle shaped in the form of praying hands, which burns the sculpted fingers when lit. In these cases, the aesthetic item serves two purposes and two masters, sometimes in conflict. Paintings and sculptures of this kind are consequently confused, impure, and deficient in the expression of taste.

§51: POETRY, HISTORY, AND TRAGEDY

Poetry is a challenging art for Schopenhauer's theory, given how he condemns abstract concepts for their metaphysically empty, merely summary quality. Poetry is constituted almost wholly by abstract concepts and yet he locates poetry as the highest art, side-by-side with music, following a long tradition that respects poetry as such. According to Schopenhauer, poetry is the best art for expressing the Platonic Idea of humanity in its most explicit multi-aspectedness, and hence, in its truth.

Schopenhauer's solution to poetry's inherent tension between abstract concepts and Platonic Ideas is to attend to the style in which the concepts are combined in poetry. He compares poetry to chemistry, stating that the poet's task is to precipitate concrete perceptions through word sequences, just as the chemist can precipitate solids in a solution by combining liquids that are initially clear and transparent. Thinking poetically involves being sensitive to the clusters of associations that each concept carries along with it, and the ability to combine concepts whose respective clusters of associations, when blended, yields a wealth of supplementary and imaginative thought. Allegorical thinking is consequently acceptable in poetry, although it does not work well in painting and sculpture, as he argued at the end of the last section.

Reflecting upon other modes of employing abstract concepts, and also upon the history of aesthetics, where we find Aristotle discussing the same topic, Schopenhauer reiterates Aristotle's position that poetry is a higher discipline than history. Poetry can imaginatively construct characters and situations, and can arrange them in an ideal set of relationships to portray a given theme, whereas history is saddled with the actual facts of what happened, the contingencies of actual people's characters, and the imperfections and accidents of events. As a result, history can rarely present a polished and perspicuous rendition of a timeless human theme, which is the very point of poetry.

Despite its preferred place in contrast to history, poetry nonetheless admits of different kinds, and these vary in the degree to which they can present the timeless depths of human character. Schopenhauer mentions among types of poetry, the lyric, song, ballad, idyll, romance, epic, and tragedy, and locates tragedy at the summit of poetic art. He is not the only theorist to do so—Hegel's and Schelling's aesthetics also locate tragedy as the highest spiritually oriented art—but the peculiarities of Schopenhauer's Will-oriented vision of the world motivates his evaluation. The Schopenhauerian purpose of tragedy is to describe life's pain, misery, misfortune, and absurdity in an artistically revealing, naturally appearing and non-contrived way.

Among all of the arts, Schopenhauer believes that tragedy displays his pessimistic vision of the world most effectively. Individuals, typically great ones, come into predictable conflict, if only because their respective characters and interests inevitably clash. Disaster follows, as these individuals—all composed of the single Will that underlies everything and that feasts upon itself within in the realm of the principle of sufficient reason—attack each other and die.

For the audience, tragedies hold up life in a mirror for all to see with a measure of detachment and understanding. They reveal the conflict-permeated vision of the spatio-temporal world which Schopenhauer presents in his philosophy, and they allegedly stimulate the proper reaction to this world as Schopenhauer conceives of it, namely, profound resignation—a resignation that entails the denial of one's urge to participate in the spatio-temporal world.

§52: MUSIC AS THE PAINLESS FORM OF ONE'S INNER BEING

Schopenhauer concludes Book III and his overall treatment of aesthetics with an interpretation of the nature of music—an art that does not fit into his earlier discussions and which importantly plays a transitional role as we move from Book III to Book IV. According to Schopenhauer, music does not reveal Platonic Ideas, but as a "copy" of Will, reveals Will itself.

If we recall the holistic vision of the set of Platonic Ideas that range from inorganic matter to humans, and add that these Ideas are the immediate objectifications of Will, some of Schopenhauer's observations about music's unique quality will make more sense. Just as Will objectifies itself into a hierarchy of Platonic Ideas, music's elementary structure symbolically expresses that act of objectification and resulting hierarchy in three ways: (1) music is structured along a range from bass notes, to middle notes, to high notes, (2) music is structured according to the tripartite levels of bass, harmony, and melody, and (3) when we pluck a single note on a stringed instrument, the note resonates with a series of overtones ranging from low to high. We thus have a series of related levels in musical structure that symbolically accord with the hierarchy of the immediate objectifications of Will, the Platonic Ideas. In view of the analogies and of its capacity to express human feeling, Schopenhauer appreciates music as being a "copy" of the Will that objectifies itself into the hierarchy of Platonic Ideas.

Schopenhauer's association of the plucking of a single note and its musical overtones with the spectrum of Platonic Ideas might have been inspired by his reading of the Māndūkya Upanishad, which locates a single sound at the core of reality in a poetically comparable way. In the Brahamanic case, the spectrum is not of Platonic Ideas, but of levels of consciousness that range from the ordinary waking state (A), to the dream state (U), to the deep dream state (M), to the ultimate state (AUM). When chanting the sound "AUM" (or "OM"), the chanter symbolically runs through the range of conscious states from ignorance to enlightenment. This matches how the plucking of a bass note symbolically runs through the hierarchy of Platonic Ideas via the overtone series that the vibrating string emanates.

Enhancing his exposition, Schopenhauer describes music as a temporal art that has no spatial or causal features. As it is experienced within the parameters of the principle of sufficient reason, time alone is its form. This exclusive limitation to time matches the "thin veil" of time, independent of space and causality, through which in Schopenhauer's key argument in §18, we experience Will, as it presents itself though our bodies.[33] Music is thus the artform closest to our direct apprehension of the thing-in-itself, and this is a further reason why Schopenhauer refers to music as an immediate reflection or copy of Will itself (*unmittelbar Abbild des Willens selbst*).

When developing the analogies between the inner being of humans and music, Schopenhauer attends to the nature of melody, noting how the different kinds of melodies—some direct, some wandering, some in major keys, some in minor keys, some long, some short, some resolved, some unresolved, etc.—are isomorphic with the ways we can feel. The structure of music in its tensions and resolutions matches the various structures of human feeling. Sad music embodies the structure of how sadness feels, and the same follows for music that expresses joy, pain, sorrow, peace, merriment, and so on. Music embodies the forms of human feeling.

Insofar as music embodies only the *forms* of feeling, however, it omits the particular experiences that cause the feelings. Music that expresses anguish and pain, leaves out the screamingly painful experiences of particular individuals who feel such anguish and pain. Just as classical Greek sculptures of human bodies are not individual or personally specific, the musical expression of feeling is not personally specific, but is universally oriented. Music expresses anguish *itself*, pain *itself*, sadness *itself*, etc., and allows us to understand what sadness is, as opposed to being emotionally consumed unreflectively in sadness. Music allows us to apprehend what Will is, and what philosophy is trying to express in concepts, and which we can now feel in music directly, but painlessly, owing to the abstractive nature of musical form.

We can now appreciate the gradual advance Book III makes toward the experience of the inner being of people, and of the world as a whole, which is now appearing in an abstracted, painless form through music. Book III begins with the apprehension of the Platonic Ideas of inorganic individuals, moves on to those of plants and animals, and then within the context of the human being, begins anew with the Platonic Ideas of the human being's outer sculptural form, only to progress through painting to poetry, to arrive at the inner world as presented through imaginatively arranged abstract concepts. Advancing conclusively to music, we enter into our inner being to a greater depth, virtually touching Will itself as it is in itself.

Schopenhauer observes that musical experience constitutes an endpoint for some, where Will, or reality, is touched upon revealingly, and touched upon in a painless way. The result is an experience of tranquillity and a short-lived measure of salvation. There is no explicit denial of Will involved in music, but only a softened, painless experience of Will, contrary to how one ordinarily experiences it in the ever-circling mode of desire, frustrations, attainment, boredom, and renewed desire and frustration.

What is lacking is a fuller, more realistic appreciation of Will as thing-in-itself, where we enter more concretely into its manifestations as the inner life of people. To reach this next level, we must enter empathetically into the actual experiences of humans that constitute their sadness, joy, disappointment, and so on. Only at that point will we understand what the Idea of humanity is in its concreteness, and how morally repulsive its manifestation is to Schopenhauer.

It requires a great imaginative effort to understand what the consciousness of humanity itself is like in all of its detail, not as an abstraction in the way music presents it, but as a full-blooded reality, where the experience would be of the mind behind the "one eye" that looks out through every living thing. Upon arriving at that distant point, one would come as close as possible to understanding one's transpersonal being as Will, insofar as it is instantiated within the field of spatio-temporal individuals. Along this path is where moral awareness enters into the picture, as Schopenhauer will now describe in Book IV, the final division of *The World as Will and Representation*. To mark this transition, he presents the image of St. Cecelia, as Raphael portrayed her, setting down her musical instruments and looking upwards toward yet another, even higher, realm.

We began our presentation of Book III by observing how it parallels Book I insofar as both books concern themselves with the world as representation, either as subject to, or as relatively independent of the principle of sufficient reason. To appreciate the underlying religious atmosphere of Schopenhauer's philosophy, we can observe how he concludes Book I and Book III with Christian imagery. Book I concludes with an image of Jesus; Book III, with one of St. Cecelia. Book IV—the book to which we will now turn—itself contains a memorable set of Christian images, and it concludes with references to Hindu, Buddhist, and Christian mysticism.

STUDY QUESTIONS

1. Explain how Schopenhauer defines beauty, and why he would accept the idea that a toad or mosquito can be beautiful.
2. What is the special capacity of the artistic genius, according to Schopenhauer, and how is this related to the purpose of art?
3. What reservations does Schopenhauer have about the traditional hierarchy of genres in academic art, which locates landscape and still-life painting at the lower levels, and history painting at the top?
4. Why does Schopenhauer locate tragedy as the highest art, among those arts that display Platonic Ideas?
5. Why does Schopenhauer locate his theory of music at the very end of Book III? How does it serve as a transition to Book IV?

SECTION 5. BOOK IV, ETHICS AND ASCETICISM, §§53–71

§53: AESTHETIC AWARENESS AS THE WAY TO PHILOSOPHY AND ETHICS

Schopenhauer begins Book IV with some reflections on the nature of philosophy and on his own philosophical method—a method which issues from a relatively time-free awareness—as it contrasts with the methods of Kant and Hegel, which rely respectively upon Aristotelian logic and dialectical reason. Anticipating Karl Marx's well-known lines from 1845— "Philosophers have only interpreted the world in various ways; the point is to change it"—Schopenhauer agrees that philosophy can only interpret, explain, and intellectually clarify what we have experientially before us.[34] Just as studying philosophical theories will not by itself give birth to philosophical visionaries, neither will an accurate aesthetic theory produce great artists, nor will a good moral theory necessarily increase the number of noble people. With such sober observations, he turns from the aesthetic theory of Book III to the philosophy of human activity, which he refers to as "practical philosophy" or "ethics."

Schopenhauer distinguishes the kind of ethical theory he will be presenting and advocating—one grounded in experience and issuing from the question of whether existence itself is valuable or not—from Kant's ethics. His theory will not be advancing, as did Kant, a theory of duty, nor will it be formulating a procedure to specify moral principles. Neither will the theory use reason to speculate about the foundations of morality that lie beyond the realm of possible experience. Abstract concepts will not be among the core items in Schopenhauer's ethics.

Schopenhauer also contrasts his philosophical method from the historical style of philosophizing that Hegel represents, offering a curious and thought-provoking argument against Hegel and historically centered philosophizing in general. According to Hegel, human history has been developing, and continues inevitably to develop, toward an ideal cultural condition that is thoroughly rational, self-conscious, and free. In the ancient oriental world, as Hegel notes in his lectures on the philosophy of history, the general recognition was that only one person was essentially free, for example, in Egypt, the Pharaoh. In classical Greece and Rome, some people were among the free, as citizens were distinguished from slaves; in contemporary times and in light of the French Revolution, we now realize that all people are potentially free and equal to each other as humans.[35] He accordingly perceives across history, a logical progression in freedom from "one," to "some," to "all," as is found in formal tables of logical judgments. This defines one strand of the underlying logic that Hegel believes informs the course of human history.

Schopenhauer disagrees with theories that postulate some rationally structured goal that human society is supposedly developing toward and is expected eventually to reach, maintaining that if time is infinite, then an eternity has *already* passed. If an eternity has already passed, then everything that has been in a process of becoming would have already become what it had been aiming to become. It consequently makes no sense to conceive of ourselves as presently in the midst of a developmental process toward a thoroughly rational condition. As far as Schopenhauer can see, the spatio-temporal world consequently involves nothing more than waves upon waves of individuals that eternally reiterate themes that issue from a timeless array of Platonic Ideas.

Although Schopenhauer admits in §28 that relationships of priority between the timeless Platonic Ideas themselves give rise to a historical sequence of development (e.g., the Idea of soil in its timeless relationship to the Idea of a tree, necessitates that spatio-temporal instantiations of soil occur prior to spatio-temporal instantiations of trees), it does not follow that although instances of soil must precede instances of trees, that trees will always prevail thereafter as existing beings. In due time, the trees will die, perhaps the soil will remain, and earth will return to an inorganic condition before, as we now believe, it is reabsorbed into the eventually expanding sun.[36]

In light of these considerations, Schopenhauer sets forth his own philosophical method, using the same phrasing with which we are familiar from his description of aesthetic perception. To achieve philosophical—and also moral—insight, it is essential to look beyond the "when," "why," "where," and "whither" of things, and to consider only the "what." As does aesthetic perception, which is Schopenhauer's paradigm for attaining this kind of extraordinary, relatively time-free awareness, philosophical and moral insight also involves the apprehension of timeless realities by means of a pragmatically disengaged state of mind.

With respect to freedom, Schopenhauer recognizes only the freedom of Will, for the universe is nothing but Will and as Will is thereby self-determining. Insofar as anyone in particular is "free," this freedom can only be conceived as the act and activity of Will itself, whereby one regards oneself as the manifestation of Will, or as reality being oneself. Significant here is Schopenhauer's insistence that there is "nothing" besides Will, for if there were, then Will would not be free and autonomous. From our existence as self-conscious beings, Schopenhauer draws the implication that the world as representation is Will coming to self-knowledge—a proposition he believes condenses the entirety of his philosophy.[37] Furthermore, if we are to speak coherently of Will being free, autonomous, and almighty, as Schopenhauer explicitly does, then reality must be Will through and through, with no other dimensions, hidden or explicit, that are not Will.[38] This important point will come up later when we consider Schopenhauer's references in §71 to mysticism and the denial of the will-to-live in connection with some of the tensions it creates within his philosophy.

Book IV's subtitle is: "Upon Arriving at Self-knowledge, the Affirmation and Denial of the Will-to-Live." In a nutshell, Schopenhauer's view is that Will unconsciously objectifies itself as the world as representation, comes to know itself through some of its human objectifications, discovers itself to be the source of endless suffering, and in reaction to this self-knowledge, acts to annul the suffering it manifests as the world of representation. The image compares to someone who proudly explores his or her family history, only to become morally horrified to learn that its most respected members were notorious murderers. Repulsed, the person then devotes his or her life to setting right the wrongs for which the family was responsible. Within the Schopenhauerian context, this translates into acting in a way that denies the egoistic, aggressive tendencies of Will's manifestation in phenomena, once one realizes what Will is. Schopenhauer refers to this cosmically repentant, self-negating activity as the denial of the will-to-live (*die Verneinung des Willens zum Leben*).

§54: LIFE-AFFIRMATION, COURAGE, AND IMMORTALITY

As we know, Schopenhauer maintains that reality is essentially a timeless being, constituted, as far as we can be aware, by Will that objectifies itself into a set of Platonic Ideas. Furthermore, he follows Kant in broad outline by admitting that human experience is always in time, and that the form of time renders it impossible for us to know absolutely and unconditionally what reality is like. Unlike Kant, however, Schopenhauer believes— at least in the majority of his discussions of this issue—that we nonetheless apprehend the thing-in-itself through a "thin veil," and since the veil is "thin," we have a fairly clear apprehension of the thing-in-itself, which he subsequently characterizes as Will. His key arguments are in Book II, beginning at §18, as we have seen. Schopenhauer's main position comes through once again in §53, when he states as the encapsulation of his philosophy that the world as representation is "nothing more" than Will's self-knowledge.

Here in §54, Schopenhauer explores the sense of time that is most appropriate for apprehending the timeless reality that is Will. His view is that when we feel as if time is standing still— he calls this the *nunc stans*—or when we feel, similarly, that only "now" or only "the present" fundamentally exists, we are temporally situated in a more metaphysically enlightened state of awareness. A vision of the world issues from this relatively time-free state of mind, and this section develops that vision is some detail.

Will immediately objectifies itself into the set of Platonic Ideas, and as we saw in §32, he closely identifies Will with the Platonic Idea, differentiating them only insofar as a timeless subject differs from a timeless object of which it is the objectification. This reflects how a timeless "I" would think of itself and recognize itself in the timeless object that it projects and apprehends as itself, as in the Upanishadic phrase, *tat tvam asi*, "that is *you*."

When Will further objectifies itself into the spatio-temporal world through the lens of the Platonic Ideas, it assumes the form of a fundamental "will to exist," and at higher levels of objectification, a "will to live." This will-to-live is a constant presence that permeates the biological world, and is the inner drive of all living things, past, present, and future. The will-to-live is Will as manifested in dinosaurs, now long extinct, it is Will that animates us presently, and it is Will as manifested in all future generations. The will-to-live is the eternal chorus of life, whenever and wherever there are living things.

To feel at one with this timeless will-to-live—to feel it surging through oneself—generates a feeling of immortality, for indeed, feeling this will-to-live is to apprehend a fusion between one's individual self and "life itself" that transcends any particular individual, finite, fleshly, generating, and corrupting condition. Within this perspective, one's own eye is felt to be the universal eye that has always looked out, and that will always look out, from all life.

Schopenhauer refers to this timeless feeling as the "complete *affirmation of the will-to-live*" (die gänzlichen *Bejahung des Willens zum Leben*). The feeling says "yes" to life, as one feels the flow of energy within oneself as the eternal flow of energy that surges through everything, as the fear of death dissolves, as courage inflates the soul, and as one realizes that the death of the individual is illusory in contrast to the energy of life that erupts continually, generation after generation, and that constitutes one's true being. The feeling is of an "eternal present," where the constant recurrence of life itself becomes one's own universal life, and where one feels like a god, eternally recurring. The complete affirmation of the will-to-live is a superhuman and universally natural feeling, in sum.

This is all contained in Schopenhauer's §54 characterization of the person who adopts a relatively time-free perspective on life—a perspective that is built upon the aesthetic attitude which can reveal the timeless beauty in things, but which is here focused squarely on the will-to-live as a timeless energy, more closely aligned with the art of music. The resulting feelings of power, courage, immortality, and eternal presence, emanate from this relatively time-free way of contemplating the world.

Schopenhauer's initial characterization of the complete affirmation of the will-to-live, or of saying "yes" to life, is alluring, given the metaphysical knowledge, courage, heightened energy, and sense of immortality it provides.[39] Schopenhauer's surprising remark is that this highly inspiring, hope-restoring attitude arises in someone *who has not yet come to know* a deeper truth, namely, that constant suffering is essential to all life. He finds it morally repulsive that the will-to-live with which one timelessly identifies, is the murderous energy that generates the world's suffering and that flows through himself. To him, a precondition of experiencing the positively superhuman and supercharging attitude of life affirmation is to be morally insensitive to the widespread suffering in the world that traces back to one's very essence. On moral grounds, Schopenhauer cannot condone a life-affirming and self-affirming outlook.

§55: FREEDOM, DETERMINISM, AND CHARACTER

Accepting Kant's view that our freedom issues from a dimension independent of space and time, Schopenhauer maintains that Will acts variously to determine the multiplicity of individual human characters, all of which are themselves timeless. As timeless, our individual characters are fixed, determining us to be born with certain leading desires that characterize us as the individual personalities we happen to be.

Alternative avenues are possible for realizing our inherent desires, but our overall character remains the same throughout. At different times in our lives, we will have different degrees of knowledge, and relative to these differences, different paths toward the same end will present themselves. A need for fame and recognition can be realized in an assortment of ways, for example, depending upon the circumstances and state of self-knowledge.

This account of character implies for Schopenhauer that there is a single tendency that each person has, definitive of his or her personality, and that during the course of life, a person can realize that tendency more or less effectively, as a seed might grow into a strong or weak tree, depending upon whether it has enough water, sunlight, and nourishment. Since humans apparently have more self-control than animals or plants, Schopenhauer understands personal development in terms of a movement toward acting as consistently as possible with who one is. In the end, the person would act with a single, directed, characteristic will that reflects who the person timelessly is, and acquires "character" thereby. Upon acquiring character and consequently becoming what one is, a measure of self-coincidence and contentment follows.

A curious aspect of Schopenhauer's discussion arises when he states that it is possible to act in a manner that is more noble or more selfless than how one's character would ordinarily dictate.

When this happens, there will be some feelings of uneasiness about the uncharacteristic behavior, and an inevitable return to balance with the resumption of one's more typical egoistic activity. In this respect, Schopenhauer believes that each person's ethical quality is fixed, and that acting authentically is best, as opposed to acting inconsistently with our character, even if acting out of character would be more virtuous.

With respect to moral responsibility, then, rather than blame or praise a person's specific act, one would fundamentally blame or praise the person for who he or she is. We can also reasonably blame a person for not having acted in character well, that is, for having taken the wrong path to self-realization, had the knowledge been available to that person which would have led them to act more in character. A related idea is to blame a person, not, for having failed to act well in accord with how humans ought to behave, but for having failed to act well in accord with what that person's own character dictates.

This notion of responsibility might sound peculiar at first, but if we reflect on how individuals in Greek tragedies ascribe responsibility to themselves, Schopenhauer's notion of moral responsibility reveals its classical roots. Oedipus did not know that when he killed his father, that the man was his father. Neither did he know that when he married his mother, that the woman was his mother. From a contemporary moral standpoint, Oedipus should not be blamed, nor should he blame himself for acts of parricide and incest, since he had no idea who the people involved were. Yet upon discovering these actions of his, Oedipus blamed himself terribly, for he conceived of himself simply as having done these things, whether or not he was in a state of ignorance concerning the details.

§§56–59: LIFE-AFFIRMATION IN THE SHADOW OF A SUFFERING-FILLED WORLD

After describing how each of us is an intelligible character that inevitably plays out its inherent desires in the spatio-temporal world, and prescribing how we can be true to our character to achieve a measure of satisfaction, Schopenhauer observes that the achieved satisfaction of living in character remains empty nonetheless. If we survey the hierarchy of living beings and observe how nervous systems gradually articulate into higher levels of complexity, it becomes evident that increased suffering accompanies the increase in physiological complexity. With our added capacity to think in abstract concepts that illuminate the past and the future, and that carry along with them increased worries, regrets, and fears, the hierarchy arrives at us humans— beings who, among all living things, seem to suffer the most.

Human existence is the highest manifestation of Will, and it exemplifies how Will's objectification only leads to greater suffering. With this realization, Schopenhauer recalls some of his reflections from §38, where he introduced the images of Ixion, Tantalus, and the Danaids to illustrate how in human life, suffering predominates, with only brief measures of relief. At the end of §56, Schopenhauer accentuates this idea with the assertion that, in essence, *all life is suffering* (*alles Leben Leiden ist*). This consideration now enters into the discussion for the sake of drawing a contrast to the earlier, superhuman image of complete life-affirmation, courage, and the sense of immortality that appears so attractively in §54. Rather than urging life-affirmation, Schopenhauer turns toward a morally motivated, self-punishing, and repentant denunciation of life, or what he calls the denial-of-the-will.

Section 57 consequently develops the vision of the world of representation as an inherently suffering world. We pursue the things we desire, and upon attaining them, it is not long before we begin to pursue another object of desire. During the interim there is a lull and an eventual feeling of boredom, and soon thereafter, an effort to relieve the boredom by aiming to satisfy newly promising desires.

Schopenhauer's estimation of human life is that most people expend their lives satisfying their desires fruitlessly, as a dog would chase its tail, not realizing that the desired items are like sand castles that are destined to dissolve. Adding to the discouraging situation, even the majority of those who are able to transcend the world of desire—among them are the artistic geniuses—are also such sensitive people by nature, that they suffer even amidst the joys and short relief of apprehending timeless objects and feeling time itself stand still.

In these more self-aware individuals, the pendulum-like swaying between unsatisfied longing and satiated boredom eventually leads to a more elevated state of mind where the compulsions of ordinary life are seen for what they frustratingly are. The initial reaction to the pressure to satisfy desire, to the subsequent boredom, and to the associated need for empty entertainment—as can be seen when people play cards, taunt animals in the zoo, and write graffiti into the walls of precious buildings—is to feel melancholy slowly seep into one's soul. This is the experience of someone who realizes as a metaphysical truth that he or she is Will, and who feels the powerful energy this is, but who also appreciates how as manifested, the will-to-live eternally produces suffering, and who begins to feel miserable as a being that not only inevitably produces suffering, but which also must bear the suffering it generates, since all is one.

Although all is Will, and although Will is constant striving, it might still appear that happiness resides in the condition of worldly satisfaction, where the satisfactions provide some relief from the pressures of the Will. This kind of happiness does not endure, however, since new objects of desire emerge to pull us along once more. In this regard, Schopenhauer notes in §58 how in view of daily life's inability to satisfy our throngs of desires, and in light of how empty and superficial life subsequently becomes, the lives of most people are both tragic and comic. From a distance and seen as a whole, the lives are tragic. When seen close up, as people find themselves immersed, for instance, in bickering over trivialities, human life appears to be a sad joke.

Upon dimly realizing the emptiness, frustration, and superficiality of actual life, Schopenhauer hypothesizes that the common reaction is to create imaginary worlds populated by demons and gods. By becoming absorbed in offering sacrifices and prayers, making pilgrimages and such, one can relieve the sense of boredom and meaninglessness, create the comforting illusion of hope, and provide some escape from life's absurdity. His reflections anticipate Marx's thought that religion is the opium of the people.[40]

Adding to this, Schopenhauer describes more specifically how intense the suffering is that is spread around the world. After commenting upon how irrationality and perversity predominate over nobility and wisdom, how dullness and tastelessness in art prevail over inspiration and genuine taste, and how wickedness and fraudulency in human social activity dominate over compassion and honesty, he reminds us of pain-filled environments such as hospitals, prisons, torture-chambers, battlefields, places of execution, and the living quarters and workplaces of slaves.

To appreciate Schopenhauer's horrific vision, we can try to imagine the suffering of all the people throughout history who have been burned at the stake, crucified, shot with projectiles, blown up, hung, or drawn and quartered, collected into a single consciousness, or single being that endures all of this suffering at once. Schopenhauer asks us to consider what our world is actually like *on the inside*, and he regards any view that reduces the significance of this colossal suffering (e.g., by asserting that it is justifiable and morally acceptable) as a bitter mockery of the unspeakable sufferings of humanity. This is his critical estimate of "optimism," as when the optimist asserts that the present world is the best possible world, or that in due time, the glory of God in its infinity will outshine all of the world's accumulated misery. Schopenhauer regards such optimism as a wicked way of thinking, and contrary to genuine Christian teaching.

This is not to deny that the ordinary world sometimes appears to be peaceful as a whole, sometimes beautiful, sometimes joyous, and sometimes inspirational. For Schopenhauer, this is only an appearance. It is a seductive false glitter that masks the underlying reality of suffering that flows beneath the world's objective surface, like a blistering river of lava that rages beneath a tranquil landscape. In this regard, the world as representation is like a beautiful portrait of a foul-charactered person, for indeed, Schopenhauer now attends to the world's inner character, and finds it permeated with suffering, just as when we lift a bandage and to our horror, behold a festering wound underneath.

§60: SEXUAL REPRODUCTION AND THE AFFIRMATION OF THE WILL-TO-LIVE

One's body is the objectification of Will. More specifically, it is the objectification of the intelligible character that one is, which is itself a timeless act of Will. For this reason, Schopenhauer employs the phrases "affirmation of the will" and "affirmation of the body" interchangeably. The body's natural aim is health and reproduction of the species, and from these motives, sexual impulses become the central expression of the human body's affirmation.

Schopenhauer notes generally that motives always promise complete satisfaction, drawing us on accordingly, but when their aims are achieved, their satisfaction is short-lived, and eventually new, refreshed motives emerge to draw us on toward yet another illusion that promises complete satisfaction. So it is with sexual satisfaction, the deepest motive within the sphere of the body's affirmation and the producer of the deepest illusion. Everyone is sexually driven, continually led onward by the false guarantee of an eternal happiness that resides in sexual fulfillment.

From within the sphere of the body's affirmation, Schopenhauer maintains that once a person secures a measure of security, the next natural step is toward reproduction. In colloquial terms, many people's life-plan is to secure reliable employment and then raise a family as a satisfactory endpoint. This is the highest goal within the sphere of bodily affirmation, and for many, the successful establishment of a well-paying job and a stable family provides absolute value and a sense of closure to their lives. We can imagine a proud and happy parent holding his or her child, playing contentedly, laughing joyfully and innocently with the child, and feeling through that activity as if her or his life has been totally fulfilled. The longer-term view of what will become of the future generations of people, and eventually, to the earth itself, does not present itself, nor does the essential frustration and suffering inherent in human life reach any explicit thematization. Within this limited perspective, the genitals positively symbolize life's meaning, for they symbolize eternal life and eternal creation, since the will-to-live is timeless.

Within a broader perspective, Schopenhauer situates his interpretation of the act of procreation within his account of the nature of Will, where the latter is conceived not as a celebrated force of eternal life, but as an eternal lack and endless striving. Aside from the inevitable experience of personal frustration, as is the case with the achievement of every motive, Schopenhauer observes that the end result of procreation—the creation of new life, which is the underlying aim of the will-to-live—perpetuates the world's suffering. Human beings suffer by nature, and humans suffer the most within the spectrum of living things, owing to their capacities for reflection and conceptualization, so the creation of new humans is an act of creating more suffering and more death, since one's children will themselves suffer and die.[41] Sex is consequently the affirmation of suffering and death, and for Schopenhauer, it is therefore an act for which we all should feel guilty.

The upshot is that, on the one hand, human beings embody the Biblical image of Adam, for they are condemned to suffering and death, precisely because they are fleshly beings with an inherent desire to maintain and reproduce themselves. Our very nature as instinctually driven, living beings is our original sin. On the other hand, there is within us the act of reflection that reveals how our instinctual nature is responsible for perpetuating suffering and death in the act of perpetuating new life. This introduces a questioning and distancing from our instinctual energies, and a subsequent renunciation of instinct and the affirmation of the body. Schopenhauer introduces in this latter context the image of Jesus, who represents for him the denial of the will-to-live and the notion of self-sacrifice—an image that he will develop in later sections.

The conclusion of §60 reveals the immense difficulty that Schopenhauer is facing here, as he observes that the affirmation of the body is nothing more than Will objectifying itself. Since he has expressed the position that there is nothing but Will, that is, Will is reality, then the thought of escape from Will's objectifications is tantamount to the paradoxical thought of escaping from reality itself.

The tragedy and comedy of human existence is nothing other than Will objectifying itself, and since this is the case, Will *itself* bears the suffering, bears the responsibility, bears the guilt, and within the enlightened human being, observes itself as such. Will does this all to itself, and hence, there is nothing but a self-enclosed circle of reality within which millions of acts of objectification and feelings of guilt transpire. This self-enclosed circle reveals an inherent *eternal justice* within the universe, for there is only one being that bears the different sides.

§61: EGOISM AND WORLDLY CONFLICT AS THE EXPRESSION OF AN ORIGINAL DISCORD IN WILL

Having disclosed how the affirmation of the body produces suffering and death, Schopenhauer now considers the situation more fundamentally, with an aim to reveal the source of all conflict. He locates this in the nature of reality itself, observing an original discord in Will, owing to how it immediately objectifies itself into a set of Ideas that are in conflict with one another. The Idea of the anteater conflicts with that of the ant, the Idea of the Venus fly-trap conflicts with that of the fly, and so on. Once these Ideas are instantiated in space and time, the respective individuals who reflect the Ideas begin to conflict with one another.

Since space and time—the *principium individuationis*—are not features of Will as it is in itself, but are only features of the human mind requisite for empirical knowledge, the violence within the world as representation is partially due to the specific nature of the human being. Human nature is itself an objectification of Will, and so the principle of sufficient reason, of which space and time are expressions, is an objectification of an original discord in Will—a discord that we also apprehend as the timeless hierarchy of Platonic Ideas.

As we ascend through that hierarchy, the inner nature of Will becomes more manifest. The intelligible characters of human beings are at the apex, so the original discord in Will shows itself most clearly in us. Our own sense of egoism—and Schopenhauer refers to egoism, considered generally, as the starting-point of all conflict—expresses the original discord in reality as a whole.

As we saw in Schopenhauer's discussion of the sublime, the human being displays a further discord in having a dual self-awareness whereby each of us, on the one hand, regards himself or herself as an infinitesimally small physical body among the innumerably billions of objects in the universe, and on the other, as a subject of knowledge that has the very physical universe in its mind as a set of its own mental images. From the standpoint of the subject of knowledge, we each feel as if we are the center of the universe, and we feel this way despite how we recognize ourselves physically as virtually specks of dust in the larger scheme of things. The immediate presentation of beings other than ourselves is yet another of our mental representations, and hence, they appear as beings that depend on us for their existence. This further accentuates our egoistic feeling.

Furthermore, the immersion of our consciousness in space and time minimizes the intensity of our awareness of the identity of Will as the inner nature of other representations, and so *prima facie*, we face those other individuals as aliens, and as potential threats to our egoistic self-certainty. We are therefore disposed to control or annihilate these others. In the original human condition, then, given our dual knowledge of ourselves and our initial entrenchment in the spatio-temporal world, we are in the midst of a *bellum omnium contra omnes*, a war of all against all.

§62: RIGHT, WRONG, PROPERTY, PUNISHMENT, AND THE STATE

Prior to discussing the "denial-of-the-Will"—the condition where one minimizes or "denies" Will's desiring and striving energies within oneself—Schopenhauer attends to the more common situation where one denies Will's expression within beings other than oneself. This is the equivalent of violent or aggressive behavior toward others.

Since all is Will, the existence of aggression reveals how Will is in a fundamental self-conflict once it objectifies itself. Within the spatio-temporal world, this conflict occurs at a fairly high level of illusion, since neither the aggressors nor the victims tend to realize that Will denied in another is the same Will that surges through the denier as well. This leads us to the threshold and sphere of "ethics," or to a context of ordinary interpersonal relationships where one distinguishes oneself clearly from other people. For Schopenhauer, ethics is concerned primarily with acting rightly or wrongly.

Having established egoism—a condition that can be called "original selfishness" or "original hunger"—as the foundational state of spatio-temporal individuals, Schopenhauer develops conceptions of wrong versus right action. The baseline is a state of nature characterized by "a war of all against all," from which, and in reaction to which, ethical relationships emerge. Assuming that as spatio-temporal beings, we are egoistic through-and-through, Schopenhauer defines "wrong" activity as occurring when one individual, in the midst of pursuing his or her egoistic desires, denies the expression of another person's efforts to pursue his or her similarly egoistic desires.

"Wrong" (*das Unrecht*) is aggression or violence against another person while in the pursuit of one's own egoistic aims. Individuals can do wrong, as well as can institutions and States. "Right" (*das Recht*), in contrast, is simply the negation of wrong, and can be ascribed to any action that does not transgress another's assertion of will. In Schopenhauer's use, the term "right" is more accurately expressed by the words, "permissible" or "alright," and the term "wrong" is more accurately expressed by the words "prohibited" or "ought not to." His theory describes what is permissible, as this is defined against what one ought not to do, namely, be aggressive. If some action does not interfere with anyone else's aims, it is permissible, no matter how strange it might be, and even if it involves abstaining from helping someone in distress. Schopenhauer is a theorist who grounds his ethics on the principle of non-interference in the lives of others, maintaining that everyone has a right to self-defense, and that in self-defense, lying, cheating, and doing violence to an aggressor are not wrong. This, Schopenhauer maintains, is the *original* meaning of "right," namely, warding off a wrong action directed at oneself.

Among wrong actions, Schopenhauer lists activities such as cannibalism, murder, physical violence, slavery, and theft. Within the context of theft, he reflects briefly on the conditions of property rights, noting that the mere declaration that this territory is "mine" (as when discovering some land during exploration, perhaps supported with weapons), gives no right to the land. Only when someone actually and significantly works on the land do ownership and property rights enter into the legitimate picture. One can lawfully acquire property through work upon the property, but one cannot lawfully seize it through a mere declaration backed by force.

Wrongs can also be done in subtle ways, as when manipulating others through lies and deception, thereby compelling others to serve one's own will, as opposed to their own. The most complete lies are broken contracts, Schopenhauer believes, and the most despicable lies are those perpetuated through cunning and trickery. He also maintains that aggression through explicit violence is a more respectable kind of wrong action than aggression through cunning, since the former at least displays physical strength, which everyone respects at a gut level, whereas the latter shows a self-degrading and despicable weakness.

Schopenhauer approaches law and the State minimalistically insofar as he believes that neither the legal system nor the State should actively seek to promote morality. Rather, they ought to establish counter-motives to aggression, and to create conditions where everyone is free to do as he or she wishes, as long as the realization of other people's desires is not interfered with.[42] The purpose of law should be to deter individuals from interfering with the rights of others. Schopenhauer conceives of punishment in similar terms, not as revenge or retribution, but purely as deterrence. He goes so far as to say that wrong inflicted upon a person, in no way gives that latter person a right to inflict wrong on the perpetrator.

These remarks are all extensions of Schopenhauer's initial assumption that each person is originally an egoistic individual within the spatio-temporal context, set upon realizing his or her desires. His position is subject to the criticism that the core idea of an isolated, self-enclosed individual conflicts the social nature of human beings. We are situated within a linguistic community from the moment we are born, and from an early age we are disposed to apprehend our caretakers with trust and sympathy, and to project animation into other things, as when children talk to their toys and treat them as living persons. There is overwhelming evidence that some features of our rudimentary psyche are not egoistic. Upon acknowledging these, and by adopting the view that "the social" is a fundamental category of "the human," one would be implicitly rejecting Schopenhauer's Will-centered formulations and explications of wrong, right, law, and the State from the very start.

Kant comes under attack in this section at several junctures, and although the spirit of Schopenhauer's criticisms might be defensible, he does misquote and miscommunicate Kant's position at one point. Schopenhauer mentions and then rejects a "Kantian" objection to his view that punishment serves a purely deterrent function. The objection is that such an account of punishment treats the punished merely as a means to an end, that is, as a tool to be used for deterrence. Schopenhauer presents Kant as stating to the contrary that a person must always be treated only as an end, and never as a means.[43] This is an incorrect presentation of Kant, however. Kant's assertion is rather that a person must always be treated as an end, and never only as a means.[44] We use people as a means in everyday activity, as when we use taxi drivers or airplane pilots to transport us from one place to another. Kant's point is that in doing so, we should always *also* treat the people used with full human respect. Schopenhauer usually has thoughtful criticisms against Kant, but in this instance he misdescribes Kant's position.

§§63–64: ETERNAL JUSTICE AS THE IDENTITY OF TORTURER AND TORTURED

Justice is imperfectly realized through the institution of punishment according to the State's laws, so the situation that remains can leave us frustrated. Many who have lived a life of crime often escape the hands of the law. The lives of virtuous people sometimes end in misery. Torturers and murderers sometimes go free.

Schopenhauer's metaphysics asserts that there is only one being, and this being is Will. This single being manifests itself in a variety of forms, beginning immediately with the hierarchy of Platonic Ideas, and then continuing its manifestation into the field of spatio-temporal individuals. Will lives equally in them all.

Now if a person were to identify himself or herself with the standpoint of Will, which is the standpoint of the person's metaphysical substance, it would become clear that every other person and thing is of the same substance. At this level of universal awareness, one identifies bodily with the cosmos as a whole, and essentially with the single energy of which that cosmos is the objectification. The physical universe is thus conceived of here, as being one's own physical body, and Will, which is the principle and energy of the whole, is conceived of as one's inmost being and truth of that body. To identify with the standpoint of Will is to step into the heart of the universe itself. Such a standpoint is uncommon, but it is an enlightened one according to Schopenhauer, and it reveals an eternal justice that permeates the world, just as in the physical world, action and reaction remain in perpetual balance.

Upon conceiving of the physical universe as one's body, and of Will as one's inner being, the world's violence takes on a different light. One person's hurting another is like the self-destructive insanity of one's own hand smashing the other, or of one's own foot kicking the other. From this perspective, the world's violence displays the quality of eternal transformation, as one manifestation of Will destroys another manifestation of Will, only to recycle into new forms, again to be destroyed by yet other manifestations of Will.

Will, the inner nature of the world, remains unchanged throughout, and the aggressive consciousness of the torturer is metaphysically the same being as the pain-filled consciousness of the tortured. The moment anyone affirms Will and enjoys the pleasures of appropriation and satisfaction, that person simultaneously affirms all acts of appropriation and satisfaction, for Will acts aggressively within the millions of beings that are its objectification. All of the world's actual and possible sufferings are one's own, for one is Will and the physical universe is one's true body.

Eternal justice consequently prevails, since there is only one being that acts as the torturer and that suffers as the tortured. The guilt of the torturer falls upon the victim, and the pain of the victim falls upon the torturer. Will itself bears all suffering and all guilt, for it endlessly feasts upon itself.

Schopenhauer asks within this context what the moral value of human beings thus happens to be. His judgment is that human value is reflected in human fate, and this fate is want, wretchedness, misery, lamentation, and death. This fate signifies for Schopenhauer, that human beings are contemptible, as their fate expresses what they essentially are.

The implication is that it is wrong to affirm Will, since the affirmation of Will produces aggression and death. More substantially, it can be said that according to Schopenhauer, reality itself does wrong—one's cosmic body does essentially what is wrong—for the objectification of Will is the objectification of violence. Schopenhauer's discussion implies further that when one assumes the perspective of Will, one enters into the suffering and collective guilt of humanity. In Christian terms, one takes on the sins of the world to become a Jesus-figure.

Schopenhauer cites some leading religious doctrines that support his vision that all is One, such as the Upanishadic *tat tvam asi*, as well as the doctrine of the transmigration of souls. According to the latter, if one hurts another being, then as an expression of justice, one will be reincarnated in the form of the being that one hurt. What one does to another, one also does to oneself, for all is One. Schopenhauer also observes in the Buddhist doctrine of nirvana, which speaks of a final escape, or extinguishing, of one's being in time, that we have the idea of enlightenment as a detachment from life-affirmation. Within his outlook, it specifically involves a detachment from both the physical and inner nature of the world itself, that is, a disengagement from the world as representation *and* from the world as Will. Schopenhauer speaks accordingly of the "denial-of-the-Will" as the effort to attain this disengagement.

In §64 Schopenhauer expresses his belief that the consciousness of eternal justice is known dimly to everyone, since we are all Will, and he cites how Christian ethics prescribes that we should not retaliate against evil by committing evil against the offender. The thought that "Vengeance is mine" (i.e., God's alone) is taken to signify that Will itself manages the moral balance through eternal justice. As an extraordinary example of this, Schopenhauer mentions how it sometimes happens that a person takes it upon himself to avenge a crime which has no personal relationship to him, as when upon learning of an atrocity in a distant land, the person travels to that land as an avenger. Schopenhauer interprets the person's becoming the arm of eternal justice as stemming from that person's awareness of himself as Will.

From a critical standpoint, we can observe that Schopenhauer refers to the collective suffering of humanity, of how we take on all of the world's suffering when we adopt the perspective of Will itself, and of how this is quite repulsive in the end. He does not lend much collective weight to the innumerable joys and satisfactions with which we would also identify, were we to become either Will itself, or more narrowly, humanity itself. The resulting state of awareness might not be wholly attractive, but neither will it be uniformly hellish, as Schopenhauer tends to describe it. If we were to speculate, the result would be more of a confused, bittersweet, irrational, almost deranged amalgam of feelings. In §68, we will see why Schopenhauer believes that in the world of representation, the pains nonetheless far outweigh the pleasures, and why the collective joys and satisfactions make little difference when deciding upon the worth of the spatio-temporal world.

§65: THE STRONGLY LIFE-AFFIRMING PERSON AS A BAD PERSON

Assuming that human beings are objectifications of Will and that as Will, people originally find themselves in the spatio-temporal world as egoistic beings filled with desire, Schopenhauer defines the terms "good" and "bad" (*gut und böse*) in reference to individualized Will. Specifically, "good" is how we describe any object or condition that suits, or satisfies, any particular desire. "Bad" is how we describe any object or condition that does not fit, does not satisfy, or thwarts, any particular desire.

On this conceptualization, what is good to one person is not necessarily good to another; what is bad to one person is not necessarily bad to another. All references to good and bad are relative to the person or situation, and there is no single or absolute good toward which everyone aims, at least in terms of specific objects desired. There is no *summum bonum* or "highest good."

Outside of all ethical systems, Schopenhauer recognizes a condition that he says could "metaphorically" or "figuratively" be referred to as the highest good, and this is the condition of the complete denial-of-the-will that he will describe in later sections. For the present, though, he continues to explore his relativistic, Will-oriented notions of good and bad.

Having already defined wrong actions as those that transgress the life-affirming efforts of others, Schopenhauer defines a "bad" person as someone who does wrong whenever the reasonable opportunity presents itself. The bad person is someone who is filled with an exceptionally powerful will-to-live, who has no compunction about transgressing the territory and wills of others, and who is usually aware of the kind of person he or she is. From a metaphysical perspective, we can now see that the very manifestation of Will is bad, and that the bad person radiates the nature of reality.

Speaking generally, people who have exceptionally strong desires also experience a high degree of frustration, for their demanding array of desires is never fulfilled for very long. Bad people are thus very frustrated people as well. This intense frustration is a kind of pain, so in an effort to alleviate that pain, the bad person can sometimes become cruel and wicked. The cruel and wicked person inflicts suffering on others for the sake of forgetting his or her own suffering; the person gloats over another person's suffering to alleviate or mitigate his or her own.

Since Schopenhauer is convinced that everyone is aware, if subconsciously, that they are a part of a larger cosmos whose energy flows through everyone and everything, he adds that even the cruellest people sometimes have pangs of conscience. These are the dim apprehensions that the tormentor and tormented are one, and the accompanying consciousness of the universal guilt and universal victimization that fall upon everyone. His discussion becomes fascinating when he reflects upon how bad people can reach a level of consciousness where they realize that they are themselves concentrated versions of the Will that permeates everything. Such people become the embodiments of reality itself in their position as complete, amoral, life-affirmers who are strong, fearless, and who have a sense of eternal life as they live in the "Now."

§§66–67: JUST, NOBLE, AND COMPASSIONATE CHARACTERS AS GROUNDED ON RESPECT AND EMPATHY TOWARD OTHERS

Turning now to the positive side of human character, Schopenhauer expresses his disagreement with theories that moralize, as well as with theories that aim to alter a person's motivation. The former, he claims, are not inspiring. Since motives are expressions of Will, however, the latter appeal to a person's self-interest and are not themselves morally grounded. Insofar as such theories also appeal to reason and argumentation, they are based on abstract concepts, which would imply implausibly that virtue can be taught. Since Schopenhauer is convinced that

virtue cannot be taught, he doubts their plausibility and effectiveness from the very start.

More to the point is Schopenhauer's view that genuine virtue
must issue from intuitive, direct knowledge, rather than from
abstract knowledge. This is the intuitive knowledge that must,
without any warning or reflection, dawn upon a person at some
point, where it is recognized that another person, and indeed
every other person, living thing, and physical entity, has the same
inner nature as oneself. This perception, this kind of empathy, is
the key to good character.

A good person consequently acts from the perception that
others are of the same substance as him or herself. This does
not imply that at a more specific level, everyone is of the same
character. Each person has a different character, and each
person's activity manifests his or her character. The quality of
the character determines the moral value of the action, but since
the same observable actions can have different motivations, it
remains close to impossible to assess the moral value of a person's activity. Moreover, the intelligible character that is being
manifested is itself difficult to discern. This moral inscrutability
applies to oneself as well as others.

Politically arranging the external circumstances such that
everyone's behaviors would appear to be moral, will not help us
determine whether people are in fact being good. If someday,
humans legally and politically organize themselves into the
perfect State, this State would still not necessarily touch upon
the inner character of its population. Members of a perfect
State might behave well, but this behavior would not itself imply
that the people are good, since selfishness could underlie the
behavior. Attention to the construction of such a State is consequently not on Schopenhauer's mind, since he believes that
legalities and politics remain on a superficial level of human
life, and do not penetrate to the more important spiritual and
existential issues that people face. His philosophy does not
significantly concern itself with political philosophy for this
reason.

A person who is careful not to interfere with other people as
he or she pursues the satisfaction of desire is a "just" (*gerecht*)
person, according to Schopenhauer. Such a person would recognize himself or herself in other people, and would not interfere

with others insofar as he or she would not like to suffer aggression. A just person lets other people live freely, as he or she would like to be allowed to live freely.

This is a step beyond the attitude of the egoistic person who disregards the presence and desires of others as they pursue their satisfaction, and who, acting badly, does not hesitate to push them aside, if they stand in the way of his or her own satisfaction. The just person might even tend toward voluntary poverty, as his or her needs become minimized in contrast to the sea of desire that the surrounding population manifests. The just person tends to take less, so that others might have more. Empathy is nonetheless not pronounced in the just person, since the just person is only trying to maintain a fair balance between his or her wants and those of others, retaining a substantial sense of individual self.

As the awareness of the identity of oneself with others increases in intensity, we arrive at the "noble" (*edel*) person who does not merely regard other people with the respect that is accorded to himself or herself, but comes close to feeling the suffering of others, as if it were his or her own. This takes us to a more intense level of identification with others, and precipitates noticeably selfless behavior.

The good conscience associated with just and noble people stems from their apprehension of their identity with the rest of the world. The feeling confirms this metaphysical identity and enlarges the noble person's sense of self in a satisfactory way, as he or she develops a friendly attitude toward the world, accompanied by a uniform and serene disposition. The Upanishadic phrase, *tat tvam asi*, expresses this noble attitude well, and Schopenhauer cites it at the end of this section to indicate the linkage between good personal character and the metaphysical insight that all is One—an insight that arises when we penetrate through the *principium individuationis* and apprehend a timeless and spaceless reality. The more we see identity between ourselves and the world, the more magnanimous we become. Morality aligns with identity; immorality, with differentiation.

At the highest point of goodness, as Schopenhauer describes in §67, a person will feel the suffering of others as if it were his or her own, and will make personal sacrifices unhesitatingly to help alleviate that suffering. This is the compassionate and loving soul, now having been developed to the point where he or she has become a universal person who identifies with all of humanity. Behind all of this is the assumption that suffering is psychologically troubling, morally repulsive, and should be reduced as much as possible.

Sometimes compassion leads to weeping, which Schopenhauer describes as motivated by feeling sorry for oneself. One perceives a person suffering, appreciates how the person is in a pitiable condition, and then projects oneself into that situation to become that person imaginatively. The pity originally felt for the suffering person is attributed to oneself insofar as one identifies with the person. Weeping occurs at this point, as one imaginatively apprehends oneself as being in a pitiable condition. Weeping is consequently a matter of self-pity for Schopenhauer, and it reveals the person as having a good heart.

§68: THE DENIAL OF THE WILL-TO-LIVE

This is perhaps the most important section in *The World as Will and Representation*. As the awareness of individuality diminishes and the unity that underlies all things becomes increasingly dominant in one's outlook, a more timeless consciousness emerges that runs through several stages. As we know from Book III, there is initially an aesthetic awareness, where we apprehend timeless Platonic Ideas, and which tends toward the condition of music as expressive of the forms of internally flowing emotional states. This dynamic expression of emotional states remains formal and abstracted at the end of Book III and in Book IV we become increasingly attuned to other people's inner life in a more detailed, concrete way. This initially precipitates the "just" attitude, where one remains fundamentally egoistic, but is careful and considerate not to interfere with others. A step beyond this attitude is the "noble" attitude, where one might consider sacrificing oneself entirely for the well-being of a larger group of people. Beyond the noble attitude is the "saintly" attitude, wherein a person becomes so sensitive to the suffering of others, that any one else's suffering is felt as tantamount to one's very own.

Upon reaching this point of total compassion, Schopenhauer indicates a dramatic turnaround in outlook that follows, since the wholly compassionate person, aware that Will permeates everything, realizes first of all, that Will permeates himself or herself, and second, that Will, as a mindless, ever-striving energy, in conjunction with human nature as informed by the principle of sufficient reason, is the source of the world's suffering. The saint (*der Heilige*) appreciates that the energy that fills him or her with life is responsible for the world's endless suffering, and this is disturbing. The saint becomes one with the world's suffering by looking outward and feeling empathy with others—the saint takes on the sins of the world in this way and sympathizes with tremendous suffering—but because the flow of Will within the saint is the same suffering-causing energy that is everywhere, the saint realizes that he or she is also a being that causes suffering by nature. The saint is permeated with suffering-causing energy, and is as bad as everyone and everything else insofar as the saint affirms Will.

In conjunction with this endless suffering, and as mentioned earlier, a question can be posed about the contrasting degree of joy and happiness in the world, and whether that joy and happiness should also count significantly in the saint's realization. Schopenhauer's answer can be seen through an example.[45] If we compare the pleasure of a lion that attacks an antelope, with the pain the antelope feels when the lion's teeth tear into its flesh, Schopenhauer believes that we will all agree that the antelope's pain outweighs the lion's pleasure. By regarding all of the violence within the animal kingdom to be proportioned roughly as such, and extending the model into the human realm, Schopenhauer is convinced that in the spatio-temporal world as a whole, the pains unquestionably outweigh the pleasures. If we draw a summary assessment of the total quality of the world of representation's inner life, realizing now what that inner life is painfully like, we arrive at a nightmarish image where the world's joys are swallowed up and overwhelmed by an ocean of suffering.

It might initially sound attractive to be a person who apprehends the unity of everything and feels at one with the world. Some versions of nature mysticism present this attractiveness, since nature itself is conceived of as a humane and benevolent power. Within Schopenhauer's philosophy, however, the world's unity is Will, and Will mindlessly generates continual suffering and death. If everything is Will, and if suffering and death expresses the objectified nature of reality, then upon reaching a totally compassionate outlook, the only moral reaction is to act in such a way as to minimize the objectification of Will.

The reaction is that reality turns against itself as it flows through a morally sensitive being. The experience is of rebelling against the energies that generate suffering and death and of thereby "denying" the will-to-live within oneself. Since one is none other than Will itself, this experience is of Will turning against itself within one of its manifestations, expressive of Will's repentance and self-punishment. The practical result is an ascetic lifestyle that involves becoming voluntarily celibate and voluntarily impoverished, and according to the Schopenhauerian vision, it leads one to wage a war against reality, or against oneself, conceived as Will. Schopenhauer's paradigms of ascetic, saintly people are St. Francis of Assisi (1182–1226) and Madame Guyon (1648–1717), a central figure in French quietism.

The ascetic character refuses to condone aggression, so when physically abused, insulted, or otherwise infringed upon, the ascetic does not retaliate, but rather acts in the reverse way to what Will would naturally call for within the realm of representation. Abuse is met with friendliness, violence is met with nonviolence, anger is met with patience and love, and selfishness is met with selflessness. For the sake of alleviating suffering and death, the ascetic *does the opposite* of whatever would be appropriate to the will-to-live. The ascetic is motivated to act morally—and as we can see, act in an ideally Christian manner—not mainly from feelings of compassion or love that extend toward others who are encountered in this specific situation or that, but from feeling repulsed by the suffering-generating energy that constitutes everything and from a consequent desire to alleviate suffering.

Aside from working to alleviate suffering in others, a side-effect of adopting this reversed attitude toward Will, is the generation within oneself of a feeling of heavenly peace, cheerfulness, and serenity. The world of representation, that is, the world of violence and suffering, recedes from practical engagement as one regards the ordinary, desire-filled, and illusion-generating activities of the world with supreme detachment, similar to how one might view chess-pieces at the end of the game, or after the carnival has ended, a once fear-inspiring, but now discarded party costume.

The illusions that desire creates are now dissolved and the attractive value of the ordinary world—the world as representation, with its promises of physical pleasures and worldly satisfaction—sinks to nought. Upon reaching the position where one stands against and apart from Will itself—upon detaching oneself from the Will—one is able to observe Will as akin to a bad person who in the ascetic, comes to repent. In a sense, then, Schopenhauer thus offers us a philosophy of collective guilt and repentance, or of original sin and final salvation.

Schopenhauer regards the world as representation as Will's body, so the ascetic's disengagement from his or her own body at the microcosmic level, mirrors the larger fact that within the ascetic, Will has indeed turned against itself and has negated itself. For Schopenhauer, experiencing inner reality as having reached a point where it negates itself as desire and moves in the opposite direction from generating suffering and death, is a freedom higher than the Will's immediate freedom in its objectification into a set of Platonic Ideas and aggressive individuals. This freedom is salvation.

Schopenhauer describes the denial of the will-to-live as a condition where, within an individual, the usually thoroughgoing mechanical determination of the individual according to motives, character, physiological conditions, is met with an alternative and self-negating expression of the Will within the phenomena. Ordinarily Will manifests itself freely and immediately as a hierarchy of Platonic Ideas and spatio-temporal individuals, of which one's body is one manifestation among many. In the denial of the will-to-live, the Will's expression of freedom occurs within the spatio-temporal realm itself—it occurs within an otherwise thoroughly determined field of phenomena—and it thus acts freely in the sense of acting against the momentum of that deterministic manifold. It is the only example of free will within the spatio-temporal realm that Schopenhauer admits, and it is negatively defined. When being free, one acts against some given desire, intrusion, or violence for the sake of neutralizing the guilt-generating force of Will as it ordinarily operates to fill each physical individual with insatiable desire.

§69: SUICIDE IS NOT THE DENIAL OF THE WILL-TO-LIVE

When a person suffers terribly, either physically or mentally, and then commits suicide to still the suffering, this is not an instance of denial of the will-to-live. It is an instance of life-affirmation, for if the pain were suddenly to be relieved, then the desire to live would affirmatively surge up. It is only that in such cases, the ability to affirm life has been hindered, and insofar as the person can no longer obtain what he or she wants, the feeling of being imprisoned in a situation filled with suffering leads to suicide. Unbearable physical pain is a clear motive for self-destruction. Feelings of utter hopelessness when in physical health can motivate suicide as well. In both instances, a person's attitude retains a fundamental disposition toward life-affirmation. The person desperately wants to live, but perceiving no way to live without suffering terribly, self-destruction becomes the only suffering-relieving option.

It is nonetheless tempting to describe suicide as an instance of denial of the will-to-live, if only because life is obviously "denied," or is done away with, when a person causes his or her body to stop functioning. Schopenhauer observes that objectively speaking, however, just as any individual that ceases to be does not affect the being of the Platonic Idea or intelligible character of which it is an instantiation, the elimination of an individual through suicide does not deny, or negate, the Will of which that individual is a manifestation. Schopenhauer's notion of the denial of the will-to-live operates at a more penetrating metaphysical level. It does not refer to the killing of a living physical body *per se*, but refers to a modification of the *inner nature* of that body, with the aim of reducing the intensity of desire in that inner nature.

The difference between suicide and the denial of the will-to-live can be imagined as follows. It is as if one were a balloon filled with hot, uncomfortable air, wanted to stay inflated, but sought to be inflated with cool air, rather than the hot air that comes originally with all balloons. When cooling one's inner air, the balloon reduces in size, but it remains inflated to some extent, and still remains a balloon. In contrast, suicide compares to one's popping the balloon, because one cannot tolerate the hot air inside it. The difference between suicide and the denial of the will-to-live is the difference between killing oneself while in prison, as opposed to experiencing one's actual freedom on the day of one's release.

For Schopenhauer, the denial of the will-to-live does not occur through an act of will—one does not reflectively "choose" to deny the will. He believes that practices such as voluntary celibacy or voluntary poverty arise authentically when a person arrives at an enlightened state of mind via compassion, and when desire quiets itself within the person as a result. As one comes to feel the endless suffering that Will generates, this condition of knowledge—it is the experience of moral disgust and self-hate toward reality itself—reverses one's tendency to engage in the satisfaction of natural desires. The desires fade with the knowledge acquired. The desires are not willed away, as if one could say to oneself, "I will now decide to buy and use less, so that I can apprehend the truth better." It is rather that after apprehending the truth and achieving a certain kind of knowledge, the pleasures of material goods become less appealing on their own.

At the level of the Will itself, we can understand the act of freedom that is expressed by the denial of the will-to-live as Will's retirement into itself in a weaker form, from within the field of its manifestations, as experienced from within one of its manifestations. Why Will manifests itself as human beings that apprehend their world through the principle of sufficient reason is a question that cannot reasonably be asked. Why Will appears to minimize itself here and there—like the cooler sunspots that sporadically appear on the sun's raging surface—does seem, at least, to have a moral answer: the appearance of suffering and death is morally repulsive to the most enlightened represent-atives of its highest manifestation, namely, the human being. Will's manifestation within the enlightened human being reveals to Will, as it is in the form of a human being, that it is an intrins-ically bad energy. Will itself has no consciousness or conscience, so only human beings are in the position to realize the nature of things, and to do something to relieve suffering. Upon acting to relieve suffering, there is a feeling of liberation and the relief that one's unreflective inner being—Will as flowing through oneself in the form of raw, striving, and significantly sexual energy—has not been allowed to perpetuate more suffering and death.

In sum, Schopenhauer maintains that although ordinary suicide bears a superficial resemblance to the denial of the will-to-live, it derives from an opposing mind-set, namely, that of life-affirmation. The only kind of suicide that Schopenhauer recognizes as the expression of the denial of the will-to-live is when a person dies by voluntary fasting. In this rare instance, the suicide is a side-effect of an ascetic attitude, rather than the expression of someone who is trying to avoid suffering.

§70: THE DENIAL OF THE WILL-TO-LIVE AND THE EXTINGUISHING OF CHARACTER

Schopenhauer holds that each person is an intelligible character whose behavior in the spatio-temporal world would be perfectly predictable in principle, if the empirical character and motives were completely known. The person's freedom resides in the Will's objectifying itself into this or that kind of intelligible character. On this view, as we mentioned in §55, one would not blame a person on the assumption that the person might have done otherwise. One would blame the person as a whole, for being who they are, as one might blame a cat which had just killed a bird, merely for being a cat, from whose being issues such violence.

Schopenhauer recognizes only one peculiar situation where the fixity of the intelligible and empirical characters that Will manifests can become undermined. This is when after having achieved self-knowledge, Will turns against itself within its own manifestation as the denial of the will-to-live. He offers the example of a person who comes to realize that sexual reproduction produces more beings that suffer, and for the sake of avoiding the perpetuation of suffering, becomes through that knowledge alone, someone who no longer enjoys the satisfactions associated with sexual activity. The person's genitals might have the capacity to function perfectly for reproductive purposes, but in light of the knowledge of endless suffering—it is pure knowledge here that is doing the work—the corresponding inner life of desire that would set the genitals into reproductive action evaporates. The idea compares to how certain foods such as soft drinks, potato chips, French fries, doughnuts, and luncheon meats, although very palatable and pleasurable to consume, can become undesirable in light of knowing of how they act physiologically upon the body.

The body is an objectification of Will and the genitals are the objectification of sexual desire. The person's inner life is also an objectification of Will, but in this situation, a conflict resides within the Will that is objectified within the person: one side is motivated by sexual desire; the other side feels repulsed by it in the light of metaphysical knowledge. This, Schopenhauer states, is an example of a "real" contradiction within the Will as thing-in-itself.

To illuminate this contradiction, Schopenhauer mentions Christian doctrine, citing how the doctrine of grace captures the idea of Will being in contradiction with itself. Citing Augustine and Luther, Schopenhauer notes how these thinkers maintain that the will is not free, is determined to do evil, and that there is nothing one can do personally to extricate oneself from the situation. An act of grace from God is the only way to be saved. Schopenhauer sees this as a spiritual parallel to his view, and a religious expression and confirmation that virtue and saintliness arise from knowledge, rather than Will. His point is to show how some versions of Christianity think along lines similar to his.

Schopenhauer also mentions how his philosophical outlook is reflected in the Christian doctrines of original sin, the virgin birth of Jesus, and the main tenets of Christian ethics. As mentioned, he also associates Adam with life-affirmation, since Adam represents the condemnation of humanity to suffering and death, and Jesus with the denial of the will-to-live, owing to how such denial yields peace in place of violence, selflessness in place of egoism, and so on. This all illustrates Schopenhauer's sub-project to translate traditional Christian doctrine into a more rational, philosophical form. Seeking to coordinate his philosophy with the Upanishads as well, he adds that his theory agrees with the doctrines and ethical precepts of the sacred books of India, implicitly suggesting that his philosophy contains the leading ideas expressed more imagistically by major religions across the world.

A dramatic implication of Schopenhauer's acknowledgment that in the phenomenon of the denial of the will-to-live, Will turns against itself in the spatio-temporal world, is his claim that during the course of this contradiction, Will eliminates and transcends the specific intelligible character through which it acts. This yields a kind of rebirth into a pure knowing subject free of any specific personality, and hence, a rebirth as a being whose inner reality is free from the standard motives that drive us in ordinary life.

§71: RELATIVE NOTHINGNESS AS ABSOLUTE FREEDOM

Schopenhauer concludes *The World as Will and Representation* by developing his description of the transition in consciousness that issues from the complete denial of the will-to-live. For those who remain filled with Will, the outlook associated with the complete denial of the will-to-live is unrecognizable as having much value. From that standpoint of desire, the complete denial of the will-to-live promises a deathlike nothingness, and is consequently deemed absurd. This is a common reaction to Schopenhauer's "pessimistic" philosophy, where the charge of pessimism is condemning, devaluating, or dismissive.

Schopenhauer defends his view by distinguishing between "absolute nothingness" and "relative nothingness," stating that absolute nothingness is inconceivable, since nothingness is conceivable only in contrast to being, or to some state of being. This allows him to maintain that although it might appear that the denial of the will-to-live leads to nothingness (i.e., to death, from the standpoint of desire), from another perspective, since nothingness is a relativistic notion, it can designate a different kind of awareness, namely, a desire-free state of mind.

Schopenhauer is in no philosophical position to describe constitutively the awareness that accompanies the complete denial of the will-to-live, but he offers the thought that if we were to construct a positive conception, we should look toward the writings of mystics who have reported a kind of ecstasy, rapture, illumination, or union with God. These individuals have reached an alternative state of consciousness as a result of having adopted an ascetic lifestyle based on the denial of the will-to-live, and Schopenhauer interprets this state as being more peaceful than that which the ordinary life of desire affords.

Whether all ascetics in fact have the same kind of experiences is uncertain, and it is perhaps unlikely that they do. It remains, though, that asceticism involves denying the will-to-live. One way to interpret the Schopenhauerian end-state, then, is to conceive of it as a specific experience of freedom, or liberation from desire. When a person frees himself or herself from a debilitating addiction, a feeling of relief follows, as if a great weight has been lifted. As we have seen, Schopenhauer regards desire itself as a kind of natural addiction, so the general release from desire—and this fits with Buddhist doctrine—is understandable as yielding the satisfaction that accompanies a sense of release. Nothing positive resides in the experience *per se*, for it involves only the removal and absence of a previously existing burden. As a mode of awareness, the Schopenhauerian end-state would thus be to feel completely burden-free and carefree in relation to the world as Will and as representation.

Schopenhauer concludes *The World as Will and Representation* with the remark that although the state of complete denial of the will-to-live might look like nothing to those who are still filled with Will, it remains that our world, with all of its suns and galaxies, that is, the infinite extent of space and time, becomes unimportant to the person who has denied the will-to-live.

This unimportance can be interpreted as described above, as a condition of liberation from desire that reveals no new worlds or higher dimensions, but that provides a detached, liberated, and tranquil outlook on life, as if one were the only sober person in a world filled with intoxicated individuals, or as if one were the only nonaddicted person in world constituted almost entirely by addicts. It can also be interpreted, following the example of mystical experience, as involving a transport into a spaceless and timeless state of consciousness beyond Will and the Platonic Ideas, where new dimensions of the thing-in-itself are revealed.

Consistent with both options, this state of liberation does not reveal a personal and moral center to the universe, as would a vision of God. Schopenhauer is an atheist, so however we describe the state of consciousness that issues from the complete denial of the will-to-live, it cannot undermine his antagonism to theism, which appears throughout his writings.

This is among the reasons why suggesting that the complete denial of the will-to-live positively reveals higher and additional dimensions of the thing-in-itself—one that Schopenhauer's own association of the denial of the will-to-live with ecstatic, revelatory mystical experience tempts us to assert—is less viable than the view that the denial of the will-to-live yields only a "negative" experience, coincident with Schopenhauer's characterization of pleasure as the absence of pain.

A passage in Schopenhauer's notebooks of 1821—one that appears almost verbatim in the second edition of 1844—acknowledges nonetheless that the thing-in-itself *might* have definitions, properties, and modes of existence that are absolutely unknowable and inconceivable to us.[46] The passage appears in conjunction with Schopenhauer's claim that we apprehend the thing-in-itself through the "thin veil" of time, so for consistency's sake, it needs to be interpreted as Schopenhauer's speculation about that small space between Will-in-itself and our apprehension of it through the thin veil.

To understand the situation, we can imagine apprehending an object through a piece of colored cellophane, where it remains that although we apprehend the object clearly, we cannot say that we apprehend how the object is in itself. Two points emerge from this. The first is that in connection with this interpretive issue, there is no "earlier" versus "later" Schopenhauer involved, since the controversial excerpt stems from 1821, and was only reiterated in the 1844 publication. The second point is that one can argue that it is only for the sake of philosophical completeness, that Schopenhauer acknowledges the remote possibility that in the small gap between how we apprehend the thing-in-itself and how the thing-in-itself is in itself, there might be some substantial dimension of the thing-in-itself that is being obscured by the admittedly "thin" veil of time.

From another angle, we can regard Schopenhauer's admission that the thing-in-itself might have further, absolutely unknowable dimensions, as an effort to secure a positive place for the kinds of ecstatic and revelatory mystical experience he believes might issue from the complete denial of the will-to-live, for he does direct us to the ineffable experiences of mystics as the next step beyond what his philosophy can offer.[47] There are some good reasons to avoid this interpretive line, though. First, if the thing-in-itself is understood to harbor an untold number of hidden aspects behind the supposedly thin veil of time, then the veil is no longer thin, and this contradicts Schopenhauer's many characterizations of our awareness of Will as the thing-in-itself.

Second, not only does the hypothesis of a multidimensional thing-in-itself contradict Schopenhauer's characterizations of the thing-in-itself as self-sufficient "Will' *per se*, it undermines his philosophy. If the thing-in-itself is not substantially Will, then when the thing-in-itself is divided by the principle of sufficient reason, then there is no reason for any violence to result— the violence that is essential to Schopenhauer's world-view, and which motivates the denial of the will-to-live to begin with. Without acknowledging that the thing-in-itself is Will, the world as representation can no longer be ascribed a necessary quality of constant suffering and longing, and once we admit this, Schopenhauer's philosophy falls to the ground.

The only viable option is to assert, as we have been suggesting throughout, that the complete denial of the will-to-live cannot be understood to yield any further metaphysical knowledge. The experience involves nothing more than the great relief and tranquillity that follows from conquering a virtually all-permeating addiction.

This end-state of being absolutely burden-free coincides with the tranquil facial expressions of the figures in Raphael's and Correggio's paintings that Schopenhauer now reintroduces from his characterization of the perfect Christian consciousness at the end of Book III. In the end, he speaks as an advocate of the Christian spirit, rather than as an advocate of strict Christian doctrine. He is concerned not with Christianity as an institution or set of doctrines, but with presenting a genuine ascetic consciousness—possibly the consciousness that Jesus might have experienced—in his philosophical efforts to urge his readers to contemplate and to try to feel the inner reality of things, as opposed to attending too exclusively to their merely external, scientifically understandable shells.

In Schopenhauer's own copy of the third edition of *The World as Will and Representation* (1851), he penned in a note saying that the endpoint of his philosophy is "precisely the Pradschna-Paramita of the Buddhists," a condition beyond all knowledge, and beyond the distinction between subject and object.[48] As we can see in the penultimate lines of the text, he does not wish to identify the end-state with the Buddhist "nirvana," nor with the Hindu "reabsorption in Brahman," as he understands those ideas.

Schopenhauer's implicit reference is rather to the Diamond Sutra—a sutra popular in the Zen Buddhist tradition—so we can look here for further illumination. An important aspect of this sutra is to explain with words, how words do not capture reality, how no concept is sacred, and how the truth is revealed only through direct insight. When applied to *The World as Will and Representation* as a metaphysically revealing document, seen itself as a kind of philosophical sutra, we arrive at the position that as the world, with all of its suns and galaxies, is unimportant, Schopenhauer's own text as part of that physical universe, despite how it should be appreciated for its philosophical presentation, is only a signpost and indicator of the wordless state of mind that he refers to as the denial of the will-to-live, and which he associates with the Buddhist *Prajñāpāramitā*.

In this respect, and to foreshadow our discussion of Schopenhauer's influence on later thinkers, the conclusion of Schopenhauer's *The World as Will and Representation* anticipates the matching conclusion of Ludwig Wittgenstein's *Tractatus Logico-Philosophicus*, published just over a century later, in 1921, which also leads us to a Buddhistic point of silence and direct insight. Wittgenstein writes:

> 6.54. My propositions are illustrative in this way: he who understands me recognizes them in the end as senseless, once he has climbed out through them, up upon them and over them. (He must, so to speak, throw away the ladder, after he has climbed up it.) He must overcome these propositions; then he sees the world correctly.

> 7. About that which one cannot speak, one must be silent.[49]

STUDY QUESTIONS

1. How does Schopenhauer define "wrong" and "bad"?
2. According to Schopenhauer, what is the difference between the "just" person, the "noble" person, and the "saintly" person?
3. Why does the complete affirmation of the will-to-live generate feelings of courage, fearlessness, and eternal life?
4. Why does the saintly person deny the will-to-live?

5. Why is suicide an example of the affirmation of the will-to-live, if an act of suicide ends a person's life?
6. Does the complete denial of the will-to-live provide any further metaphysical knowledge?

CHAPTER 4

RECEPTION AND INFLUENCE

The World as Will and Representation was not a highly influential book during most of Schopenhauer's life, and it became widely appreciated only after the appearance of *Parerga and Paralipomena* in 1851, published when he was 63 years old. From the 1850s onwards, though, Schopenhauer's influence spread rapidly into the fields of music, literature, the visual arts, psychology, and philosophy, touching the minds of some of their greatest representatives. As will become evident in this concluding survey, his strongest influence has been upon musicians, painters, and writers.

To contemporary philosophical ears, Schopenhauer's theory of music is more of a historical artifact than a current inspiration, owing to its dependence upon a now unfashionable metaphysics of Will. During the later nineteenth century, when systematic metaphysical speculation in the grand style was still a common intellectual practice, his theory of music had a profound impact. Among musicians, the most well-known advocate of Schopenhauer's theory of music and of his philosophy as a whole, was the towering visionary who established the groundwork for modern music, Richard Wagner (1813–83).

The most moving idea to Wagner—as we can read in his 1870 essay on Beethoven—is that Will is an endlessly striving energy that in its higher manifestations, expresses itself emotionally as a continuum of yearning desire. When translated into sound, this yields a flow of music that holds us in emotional suspension for extended periods of time, never fully resolving, as it repeatedly transforms into new structures that perpetuate the suspense, expectation, and inner tension. Wagner's later music offers this kind of experience, for indeed, he self-consciously embodied Schopenhauer's idea of the ideal musician whose individual will reflects Will itself.

After reading *The World as Will and Representation* in 1854, Wagner developed a musical style that in its use of chromaticism and harmonic suspension, not only exemplified Schopenhauer's theory, but inspired later composers to depart from traditional conceptions of tonality. Wagner's own example paradigmatically resides his opera, *Tristan and Isolde* (1856–59), where condensed in the famous "Tristan chord"—the intervals represented by the notes, F, B, D#, G#—there is an emotional tension and suspension that is sometimes taken to represent the stylistic entrance into twentieth-century music.

Although the path from Wagner to atonal music is not immediate—it compares to how one must transform Cezanne's style of painting considerably to arrive at Picasso's, even though Cezanne contains the seeds of Picasso—Arnold Schönberg (1874–1951), a key representative of atonal music, acknowledges the importance of both Schopenhauer and Wagner in his work. References to Schopenhauer's writings occur in Schoenberg's *Theory of Harmony* (1911), and his lecture on Gustav Mahler (1914).

To appreciate Schopenhauer's presence in twentieth-century music, we need only reflect upon the expressive qualities of the atonal structures themselves, which are often grating, painful, confusing, chaotic, angry, and anxious. These express complex, unresolved feelings characteristic of both an ever-striving and ever-frustrated Will, not in a smooth and dreamy way, as we often find in Wagner, but in a more metallic, abrupt, and troubled manner, characteristic of the early-twentieth-century cultural spirit of confusion and harsh despair, not to mention of the psychological characteristics of unresolved trauma. In this regard, and despite Schopenhauer's own personal preference for Rossini and Mozart, Schopenhauer's theory of music and metaphysics unlocks the expressive qualities of the tortured soul that found their proper form of artistic expression in the twentieth-century atonal music that Wagner inspired, a full century after *The World as Will and Representation* was originally published in 1818.[1]

Insofar as Schopenhauer influenced Wagner, the latter's anticipation of the music that accompanies motion pictures also conveys Schopenhauer's presence, first, in the music of early

films, where characters are each linked with a particular identifying theme, or leitmotif, and later, in contemporary films, where
the emotional life of the characters is given a richer musical
representation, owing to the more complex ideas of harmonics
that Wagner significantly initiated. Wagner's influence—and
by implication, Schopenhauer's—also extends into film scores
that reflect the style of Max Steiner (e.g., *Gone with the Wind*
[1939]), John Williams (e.g., *Star Wars* [1977]), and Howard
Shore (e.g., *Lord of the Rings* trilogy [2001–03]). It can be said
generally that the ability to portray complex feelings in music
that we see exercised at a new level in Wagner, and that continues
today in the art of cinematic scoring, has it roots in Schopenhauer's theory of music as the direct expression of Will.

If we return to Wagner's milieu, Schopenhauer's theory of music
and life-affirmation also played a formative role in Friedrich
Nietzsche's theory of tragedy. Nietzsche's point of inspiration
occurs at §54 of *The World as Will and Representation* where—
although Schopenhauer hardly advocates the attitude—there is
a fertile characterization of the type of person who completely
affirms life. When identifying with the energies of "life itself,"
there is a surge of superhuman courage, fearlessness, inspiration,
enthusiasm, and a sense of eternal life that stimulates the feeling
that in all living things, one's life recurs again and again, as we
described in the last chapter.

Aside from the resonances that Schopenhauer's characterization of the complete life-affirmer bears to the notions of the
superhuman and eternal recurrence that figure in Nietzsche's
mature philosophy, Nietzsche's early writings rely upon the
Schopenhauerian account of life-affirmation to show how ancient
tragedy with its springtime performances, offered a metaphysical
comfort to its audiences. This stems from its ability to stimulate
audiences to identify with the energies of life itself—energies
that Nietzsche associates with the tragic chorus, and which issue
directly from Schopenhauer's conception of music as the copy
of the Will. In Nietzsche's phrasings, these "Dionysian" energies
are conveyed best through music, among all of the arts, and
from this observation issues Nietzsche's faith that Richard
Wagner's music could be invoked to revivify the nineteenth-
century European culture by inspiring a sense of oneness with
feral life forces. When Nietzsche wrote *The Birth of Tragedy*,

which contains these ideas, Wagner and Nietzsche were involved in a close friendship—a kind of father-son relationship, in fact— built upon their common attraction to Schopenhauer and music.

Schopenhauer's claim that Will is the thing-in-itself is also reflected in Nietzsche's conception of the Will to Power. Both thinkers conceive of Will as the inner reality of things, and in one instance Nietzsche, using a verbal formulation that reveals his kinship with Schopenhauer's and Kant's interest in inner realities, refers to Will to Power as the "intelligible character" of the world.[2] As in most of the instances where Nietzsche appropriates Schopenhauer's ideas, he creatively modifies Schopenhauer's original conception. With respect to Will, he transforms Schopenhauer's conception of Will as a *lack*, to one of a constant *overflow* of energy, like a burning sun, and more aptly describes it as a Will *to Power*. Whereas Schopen- hauer's conception of Will resonates with yearning, deficiency, desire, need, poverty, and thirst, Nietzsche's conception suggests flooding, excess, surplus, spilling over, emanation, richness, and radiation.

Schopenhauer's vision of the spatio-temporal world as a conflict-filled arena, nonetheless coheres well with Nietzsche's reference to *agon*, or contest, mentioned in his early writings to describe the secret of the ancient Greeks' astounding cultural strength. Again, through the notion of *agon*, the Schopenhaue- rian idea of universal war—the vicious *bellum omnium contra omnes* made famous by Thomas Hobbes—is positively trans- formed into a healthy conception of one-upmanship, love of sporting contest and triumph.

Schopenhauer's violent image of the spatio-temporal world also fits Nietzsche's mature conception of "life," which involves exploitation, injury, assault, violence, appropriation, suppres- sion, hardness, deception, an instinct for power, amorality, and dominance of the stronger over the weaker.[3] The principle of sufficient reason, as Schopenhauer describes it, is the predeces- sor to this conception, except that with Nietzsche, the violence is embraced rather than abhorred.

As should now be clear, Schopenhauer's and Nietzsche's respective thematics sometimes approximate each other in their verbal descriptions. Differences between them tend to reside in their contrasting attitudes to the value and significance of pain and suffering. Schopenhauer, who embodies traditional moral sentiments, is repulsed by the suffering-filled, spatio-temporal world and considers Will to be a poisonous force. With a less pity-oriented mentality, Nietzsche celebrates the potential health-generating properties of a cosmic energy that is similarly amoral. This contrast between Schopenhauer and Nietzsche precipitates in the attitudes of the German composer, Richard Strauss (1864–1949), who embodied Schopenhauer's ideas in some of his earlier works (e.g., the opera, *Guntram* [1894]), only later to reject them in favor of a more Nietzschean outlook, as in Strauss's tone poem, *Also Sprach Zarathustra, Op. 30* (1896).[4]

Informing Schopenhauer's influence upon both Wagner and Nietzsche is his departure from the prevailing spirit of Western philosophizing—a spirit that had until the later 1700s, accorded only minor roles to those instinctual, biological, and psychological processes that soon became characterized as "unconscious." Anticipating Schopenhauer, German romantic writers offer some striking references to the unconscious part of the mind as having an unlimited depth of meaning and as being a source of mental illness, for example Novalis (1772–1801).[5] Schelling— a philosopher of German Romanticism—also spoke of the unconscious as a metaphysical principle. Schopenhauer had studied Schelling's philosophy and he was also steeped in Kant's, which itself acknowledges hidden aspects of the psyche, locating these aspects speculatively in realms that are independent of time and space.

As we know, Schopenhauer recognizes unconscious drives as the manifestations of an inner Will at the core of things. These are present as the metaphysically motivating forces that underlie everything, and which are especially evident in the behavior of plants and animals. Predominant in this conception is the will to survive and reproduce, which directly associates life-affirmation with sexual drives. Schopenhauer states accordingly in §60 that sexual drives and interests dominate the sphere of life-affirmation, and his conception of the natural human psyche regards sexual fulfillment as among life's most promising goals. Anticipating Freud, he is among the first to suggest that our unconscious energies as embodied in our will-to-live, are fundamentally sexual.[6]

In this respect, Schopenhauer's characterization of Will as a blind striving, as nonrational, as manifesting conflicting forms, as time-independent, as amoral, and as sexual when manifested in the more complex forms of life, prefigures and compares well with Freud's conception of the "Id." This is the predominant part of the unconscious, the seat of polymorphous sexual energies and one of the leading driving forces of our behavior.[7]

The historical relationship between Freud and Schopenhauer remains unclear, since only in later years does Freud positively acknowledge affinities between his psychoanalytic thought and Schopenhauer's, and then, only with qualification.[8] On some specific points, such as the theory of repression, Freud explicitly denies having arrived at the idea through an exposure to Schopenhauer.[9] The strong coincidence in content between Freud's "Id" and Schopenhauer's "Will" nonetheless suggests that his theory of the unconscious as primarily sexual has Schopenhauerian roots.

It seems that Schopenhauer looked into the depths of his own psyche, apprehended the source of the driving, sexual, nonrational, instinctual energies that he found there, and then projected this discovery as a hypothesis about the inner nature of reality. His metaphysics of Will, which regards Will as the inner nature of the objectively presented spatio-temporal world, is a large-scale expression of having apprehended the spatio-temporal world as a macrocosmic version of the sexually driven human body, with its respectively magnified inner and outer dimensions of "will" and "representation."

Once we recall Schopenhauer's conception of natural beauty as a misleadingly pleasurable appearance that masks an unsightly inner reality, the affinity between Freud's and Schopenhauer's characterizations of human life emerges clearly. For Schopenhauer, this inner reality is Will that objectifies itself as violent, suffering, aggressive, and immoral energies within the human psyche, as well as within every other being. For Freud, this inner reality is the Id that contains the same kinds of murderous and incestuous energies. Both regard manifest, objective appearances as masking a frightening and repulsive inner reality beneath. For Freud, dreams, among other psychological phenomena, serve both to display and to hide this inner reality. For Schopenhauer, the Platonic Ideas similarly both manifest and tranquillize it.[10]

In connection with the pessimism that the image of a fundamentally violent reality can generate, Schopenhauer's influence extended to a group of pessimistic philosophers born when Schopenhauer was already middle-aged. These are Karl Robert Eduard von Hartmann (1842–1906), Philipp Mainländer (1841–76), and Julius Bahnsen (1830–84), all of whom transformed Schopenhauer's outlook to derive either more temperate (von Hartmann) or more intense (Bahnsen and Mainländer) versions of his pessimism.[11] Jorge Luis Borges (1899–1986)—who was also influenced by Schopenhauer—wrote about Mainländer in connection with John Donne's reflections on suicide, *Biathanatos* (1608).[12] As Borges succinctly describes Mainländer's view, "we are fragments of a God who destroyed Himself at the beginning of time, because He did not wish to exist."[13] In contemporary terms, and loosely stated, the Big Bang manifests God's suicide.

Within the perspectives of Wagner, Nietzsche, von Hartmann, Mainländer, Bahnsen, and Borges, Schopenhauer's influence is explicit and far-reaching. In the case of Freud, it is probably more extensive than Freud cared to admit. When we come to other figures that are frequently cited as having been influenced by Schopenhauer—this is especially the case for literary figures—it is sensible to be cautious about asserting a high degree of influence, if the author himself or herself does not readily admit to it. There are usually many influences on an author, and sometimes the influences arrive second-hand. This appears to be true of Joseph Conrad (1857–1924) according to some contemporary interpreters, where Schopenhauer's influence is present, but possibly indirect. Some researchers maintain that Conrad learned of Schopenhauerian themes mainly from other writers, and did not study Schopenhauer to any great extent.[14]

A puzzling relationship obtains between Herman Melville (1819–91) and Schopenhauer. His works contain a fair number of Schopenhauerian images and themes, and he was interested in Schopenhauer's philosophy in his later years, having at one point acquired the first translation into English (1883) of *The World as Will and Representation*, which he carefully read and annotated. At an earlier age, Melville may have become familiar with the main ideas of Schopenhauer's philosophy on a voyage to Europe in 1849 via a Professor of German at NYU named George J. Adler (1821–68), but it remains that Melville's most well-known work, *Moby Dick* (1851), was written before English-language renditions of Schopenhauer's thought and works were published.[15] *Billy Budd, Sailor* (1886), written near the end of Melville's life, does have a strong Schopenhauerian resonance, for example, Billy Budd exemplifies the good person, as Schopenhauer describes such a person in §67, so Schopenhauer's impact on this work is more evident.[16]

Thomas Hardy (1840–1928) is a related case. Many studies of the relationship between Hardy and Schopenhauer commonly accept that Schopenhauer significantly influenced Hardy. To appreciate the *prima facie* plausibility of this proposition, we need only consider the misfortune-filled tenor of his last two novels, *Tess of the D'Urbervilles* (1891) and *Jude the Obscure* (1895). Hardy admitted that he had read Schopenhauer, but added that he read other figures more extensively, such as Darwin, Huxley, Spencer, Comte, Hume, and Mill, which renders Schopenhauer's influence unclear.[17] He absorbed some of Schopenhauer's key ideas and images, but some still wonder whether Hardy's exposure to Schopenhauer remained superficial.[18]

In contrast, we know that D. H. Lawrence (1885–1930) read and annotated Schopenhauer's discussion of the metaphysics of love in 1908, and wrote most of his literary works thereafter.[19] George Eliot, who was assistant editor of *The Westminster Review* when the first English-language synopsis of Schopenhauer's philosophy was published in that journal, also absorbed Schopenhauer's ideas and as some have argued, incorporated them into her influential novel, *Middlemarch* (1869–72).[20]

Leo Tolstoy (1828–1910) began reading Schopenhauer at length in 1869 and was instrumental in having *The World as Will and Representation* translated into Russian.[21] He was also reading Schopenhauer while writing *Anna Karenina* (1873–77)— a novel which includes references to Schopenhauer.[22] Tolstoy's *The Death of Ivan Ilych* (1886), also conveys the trivialization of death, even within the context of a death in the family, as Schopenhauer could easily imagine it. In his *A Confession* (1882), which is a more personal, autobiographical work, Tolstoy also refers to Schopenhauer in chapters 6, 7, 8, 9, 10, and 12.

In 1899, Tolstoy also published a short book, *What is Art?*, where he developed a theory of art as the communication of feeling. Tolstoy's theory of art is structurally identical to Schopenhauer's, for according to both, the artist apprehends some reality (for Schopenhauer this is a Platonic Idea; for Tolstoy this is a certain kind of feeling) and then embodies that reality in an artwork as a way to transmit the exact experience to others. Along the same lines, except shifting to focus upon eternal truths that are communicated, Schopenhauer's theory of art also influenced the French symbolists of the 1860s–80s, who sought to express timeless realities in their artworks and poetry, as opposed to copying either nature slavishly or other artists derivatively.[23] On the other side of the world, the aesthetic theory of the Chinese scholar, writer, and poet, Wang Guowei (1877–1927), was also steeped in Schopenhauer's views, perhaps more sympathetically and straightforwardly than any of the individuals mentioned so far.[24]

We should also include Guy de Maupassant (1850–93) and Thomas Mann (1875–1955) on the list of major writers who Schopenhauer influenced. At one point, Maupassant refers to Schopenhauer as the "greatest shatterer of dreams who had ever dwelt on earth.[25] Mann describes Schopenhauer's philosophy as a "pitiful-pitiless coruscation of statement, citation, and proof of the utter misery of the world."[26]

As did D. H. Lawrence at age 23, Samuel Beckett (1906–89) read Schopenhauer at the relatively young age of 24, and then later at age 30, discovering in Schopenhauer's works, the greatest intellectual attempt to justify unhappiness.[27] Beckett's friendship with Emil Cioran (1911–95), yet another author whose writings embody an awareness of human futility, reveals a pair of despairing spirits who wrote under Schopenhauer's inspiration. Cioran studied Schopenhauer when young, and was impressed especially by Mainländer, as well as by Borges, when he discovered that Borges had also encountered Mainländer, as noted above.[28]

Less widely recognized, yet no less important as one of Brazil's greatest writers, Joaquim Maria Machado de Assis (1839–1908) reflected Schopenhauer's ideas in his writings. In one of the first studies of Machado de Assis's thought in English, we find a description of how Machado, explicitly invoking arguments from Schopenhauer, regards the unfortunate and painful death of a young boy as an example of the human condition.[29]

Among the leading twentieth-century philosophers, the influence of Schopenhauer upon the young Ludwig Wittgenstein (1889–1951) is most frequently cited, whose notebooks from 1916 when he was an Austrian soldier during First World War, contain a scattering of reflections on *The World as Will and Representation*. These arise in connection with Wittgenstein's concerns about humanity's meaning as he was surrounded daily by an atmosphere of lives being wasted by war. By projecting an underlying interest in life's overall significance into Wittgenstein's later works, it is possible to appreciate Schopenhauer's influence extending across Wittgenstein's corpus, beyond the close correspondence between the conclusions of *The World as Will and Representation* and Wittgenstein's *Tractatus Logico-Philosophicus*, as we noted at the end of our discussion of Book IV.[30] Also representing Schopenhauer's influence in Austria, it has been argued that Gustav Klimt (1862–1918) presented Schopenhauerian themes in his three controversial paintings that were commissioned for the University of Vienna's great hall, *Philosophy* (1900), *Medicine* (1901), and *Jurisprudence* (1903).[31]

Not all of Schopenhauer's influences are ones of which to be proud. It is a strange coincidence, but one worth mentioning, that Adolf Hitler, a schoolmate of Wittgenstein in Linz (the two men were born six days apart and occupied the same schoolroom in 1904, at age 14) also carried a copy of Schopenhauer's volume with him when he served in the Bavarian army during the First World War.[32] Hitler had an affinity for Schopenhauer's outlook and quotes him on an anti-Semitic point in *Mein Kampf* (1925–26).[33] Hitler's insistence on keeping the concert halls open during the bombing of Germany to offer an oasis of escape from war's horrors is also consistent with Schopenhauer's aesthetics.[34] As we also know, Hitler was enthusiastic about Wagner's music and outlook, and in light of how Schopenhauer inspired Wagner, it is difficult to avoid drawing Schopenhauer into the dark history of Nazism, if only in a peripheral way.

On a different conceptual dimension, there have been studies in more recent years that credit Schopenhauer with the insights that underlie the mathematical notion of fuzzy sets.[35] The connection arises in relation to Schopenhauer's discussion of overlapping concept spheres that he diagrams in *The World as Will and Representation*, §9. In relation to twentieth-century Anglo-American philosophy in conjunction with Wittgensteinian thought, it has also been suggested that one of the more influential philosophical books of the 1950s, Gilbert Ryle's *The Concept of Mind* (1949), contains a substantial number of Schopenhauerian ideas.[36]

Schopenhauer is not mentioned in Douglas R. Hofstadter's Pulitzer Prize winning book, *Gödel, Escher, Bach: An Eternal Golden Braid* (1979), but as we have seen in our presentation of *The World as Will and Representation*, §7, §27, and §39, Schopenhauer should be recognized as among those philosophers who utilize the "strange loop" structure at the very basis of their thought. In Schopenhauer, to recall, this involves the peculiarity of saying that although my mind is in my head, my head is in my mind, and although my head is in my mind, my mind is in my head. This mind-bending thought gives one extended pause, and we may conclude our present examination of *The World as Will and Representation* in the wake of that strange loop's convoluting quality, allowing it to work silently and bewilderingly as Schopenhauer intended.

NOTES

CHAPTER 1: CONTENT

1 *Manuscript Remains*, Vol. I, §81 (1813), p. 44, as well as §37 (1812), p. 24 and §15 (1809–10), p. 11.
2 Schopenhauer reiterates this idea in his notebooks of 1814. *Manuscript Remains*, Vol. 1, §213, Dresden, 1814, p. 130.
3 Urs App. "Schopenhauer's Initial Encounter with Indian Thought." *Schopenhauer-Jahrbuch*, 87 (2006), pp. 35–76.

CHAPTER 3: READING THE TEXT

Section 1. Schopenhauer's Prefaces to *WWR*, His Critique of the Kantian Philosophy, and *the Fourfold Root of the Principle of Sufficient Reason*

1 *Manuscript Remains*, Vol. 1, Teplitz, 1816, §551, p. 409.
2 *Critique of Pure Reason*, "Transcendental Aesthetic," A45/B63.

Section 2. Book I, Perceptual Vs. Abstract Representations, §§1–16

3 A revealing example is Schopenhauer's reference to the slogan within the context of his critique of Kant: "Kant's fundamental mistake is that he did not enunciate and acknowledge the proposition: 'No object without a subject' which Berkeley had laid down to his immortal credit" (*Manuscript Remains*, Vol. 2, "Against Kant," p. 462).
4 Schopenhauer's argument recalls a similar one presented by Augustine (354–430) in his *Confessions*, chapter XI. For a modern, and alternative, argument for the unreality of time influential in the history of philosophy after Schopenhauer, see "The Unreality of Time," by John Ellis McTaggert (*Mind: A Quarterly Review of Psychology and Philosophy*, 17 (1908), pp. 456–473).
5 *Critique of Pure Reason*, A26/B42 and A35/B51–52.
6 As the extreme representatives of idealism and materialism respectively, Schopenhauer mentions Bishop George Berkeley (1685–1753) and Paul-Henri Thiry, Baron d'Holbach (1723–89). See *WWR*, II, chapter I, "On the Fundamental View of Idealism," which serves as a supplement to *WWR*, I, §§1–7.
7 *Critique of Pure Reason*, A28/B44.
8 We should note, however, that the metaphysical *structure* of Schopenhauer's outlook (as opposed to the style of argumentation

he is using to arrive at this outlook, which we are discussing here) does assume an idealistic form, where an inner being, "Will," although it does not "cause" the world as representation, does objectify itself into the world as representation.

9 For a detailed study of the idea of a "strange loop," see Douglas R. Hofstadter, *Gödel, Escher, Bach: An Eternal Golden Braid* (New York: Vintage Books, 1980), and other works by Hofstadter.

10 This is Schopenhauer's own example. Here, the concept "animal" contains the concept "horse" as a genus contains its species concepts. The concept of wider scope contains concepts of smaller scope. An alternative way to conceive of the relationship of containment—one that we encounter in Kant's notion of analytic judgments—is to say that the concept, "horse," contains the concept, "animal," insofar as "horse" implies "animal," just as "bachelor" implies "unmarried." The richer concept contains the thinner concepts.

11 Schopenhauer is referring here to one of the four roots of the principle of sufficient reason that he defines and examines in his doctoral dissertation.

12 Schopenhauer elaborates on the "laws of thought" in *The World as Will and Representation*, Vol. II, chapter IX, "On Logic in General."

13 A classic in this subject from the perspective of a European student, is Eugen Herrigel's, *Zen in the Art of Archery* [1948], trans. R. F. C. Hull (New York: Vintage Books, 1971).

14 For an extended discussion of Schopenhauer's theory of humor, see Peter B. Lewis, "Schopenhauer's Laughter," in *The Monist*, Vol. 88, No. 1 (2005), pp. 36–51.

15 One of the most renowned—and for a Schopenhauerian, ill-conceived—attempts to derive all mathematical truths from symbolic logic is Bertrand Russell's and Alfred North Whitehead's *Principia Mathematica* (1910). A contemporary axiomatic treatment of Euclidean geometry was formulated by David Hilbert, in 1899.

Section 3. Book II, Will as Thing-in-Itself, §§17–29

16 Schopenhauer's position, along with his slogan, "No object without a subject," is inspired by the British empiricists, John Locke and George Berkeley. Locke maintains that the immediate objects of perception, thought or understanding are ideas (*An Essay Concerning Human Understanding*, chapter VIII, Section 8). Berkeley maintains similarly that the objects of human knowledge are ideas (*The Principles of Human Knowledge*, Section 1).

17 As a rule, when referring to "Will" as the thing-in-itself, considered in its wholeness as the principle of reality, the word will be capitalized. When referring to this Will as it is embodied or working through this or that individual in some specific situation, the word will appear in small letters.

18 In his book, *Schopenhauer* (Penguin, 1967), Patrick Gardiner
suggests this criticism, and interprets Schopenhauer's admission
that the temporal apprehension of ourselves as "will," has the dev-
astating effect of retiring the thing-in-itself "beyond all cognitive
range" (Gardiner, p. 173). The result is to reduce Schopenhauer's
position to Kant's, insofar as Kant maintains that the thing-in-itself
is unknowable and outside of any experience.

19 This double-filter image is advanced by Julian Young, in his book,
Schopenhauer (Routledge, 2005), p. 94, as an argument against
Schopenhauer, again aiming to show that Schopenhauer's position
regarding the thing-in-itself is essentially the same as Kant's.
Young also criticizes Schopenhauer's argument that we can have
insight into the nature of the thing-in-itself on the grounds that
every "act" of Will must take place in time. This is a questionable
argument, though, if one acknowledges the *prima facie* plausibility,
albeit within another philosophical framework, of God's having
"acted" to create the world, that is, having acted timelessly to create
time and space. There is a well-entrenched conception of timeless
acts in the history of Western philosophy and theology. As part
of this tradition, the notion is present in Kant's moral theory
and theory of human freedom, from which Schopenhauer's own
argument derives.

20 See Berkeley's *Principles of Human Knowledge*, Section 27.

21 Schopenhauer believes that extrasensory perception, for example,
clairvoyance, as well as magic, can be explained by assuming, as
his philosophy maintains, that our individual consciousnesses are
connected to each other at a metaphysical level. See his chapter
entitled, "Animal Magnetism and Magic" in *On the Will in Nature*.

22 Schopenhauer does nonetheless state that the existence of human
beings is the objectification of Will's arriving at the self-realization
that it is a bad energy. The subsequent denial of the will-to-live in an
ascetic lifestyle consequently represents the Will's endpoint. Will
does not consciously aim for this eventual self-negation, but it does
manifest this condition, as a plant unconsciously yields fruit.

23 Schopenhauer does not believe that presently existing individuals
recur at some future time exactly as before, over and over again.
He has more loosely and realistically in mind a constant recycling
of the same kinds of forms and the same kinds of stories, where
the contingently occurring individual differences make no real
difference. Future wars will have different people in them, but the
narratives and issues revolving around hate, fear, ignorance, and
aggression will be the same.

24 This interpretation of Will, namely, as an aspect of a multidimensional thing-in-itself, is also implausible since it requires the
thing-in-itself to embody multiplicity, given its many dimensions.
Multiplicity, however, remains within the exclusive province of the
principle of sufficient reason. Schopenhauer consequently has no

choice but to apprehend the thing-in-itself as a single, undifferentiated reality.

25 This claim can be questioned, however, since some philosophers recognize timeless logical structures that have a goal-directed quality. Hegel's *Logic* is an example.

Section 4. Book III, Platonic Ideas, Beauty and Art, §§30–52

26 In Schopenhauer's notebooks of 1814, he regards Will and Platonic Idea as identical as well, so the postulation of this identity is a persistent thought in Schopenhauer's philosophy. See *Manuscript Remains*, Vol. 1, Section 305, p. 205, Dresden, 1814.

27 One must wonder, though, if the higher-level Ideas are allegedly of deep significance and suggestive content, as Schopenhauer later states in §42, how such meanings can be present in the absence of some internal differentiation. Confirming this thought, Schopenhauer states in §48 that the Idea of humanity is "many-sided" (*vielseitig*).

28 When we discuss Schopenhauer's influence in the final chapter, we will note the coincidence between Schopenhauer's views and Freud's.

29 The word translated into English as "the charming" is "*das Reizende*," which is also sometimes translated as "the physiologically stimulating." Schopenhauer follows Kant's lead and wording here, for Kant also separates the charming quality of perceptual objects from their beauty. According to Kant, the charming pleasure (*der Reiz*) varies irreconcilably from person to person (*Critique of the Power of Judgment*, §13) and it conflicts with how he conceives of beauty, where differences in judgments of beauty are reconcilable. Although some people may like the taste of white wine, and some may not, Kant believes that this is not the case with beauty, where the satisfaction is more universally grounded, and where in principle, we can expect everyone to agree with us.

30 Stendhal (Marie-Henri Beyle), *De l'amour* [1822] (Paris: Gallimard, 1969), chapter XVII, p. 53n.

31 "Objects which in themselves we view with pain, we delight to contemplate when reproduced with minute fidelity" (*Poetics*, Section IV, 1448b).

32 The phrase occurs originally in the Chandogya Upanishad, chapter six.

33 Although restricted to single form of time, a difference is that in music, we experience a stronger sense of past-present-future, as opposed to the feeling of time standing still, which is more characteristic of the "thin veil."

Section 5. Book IV, Ethics and Asceticism, §§53–71

34 Marx's remark is from "Theses on Feuerbach" (1845), Thesis XI. The theses were first published in 1886 as an appendix to Friedrich

Engel's work, *Ludwig Feuerbach and the End of Classical German Philosophy.*

35 See G. W. F. Hegel, *The Philosophy of History* (New York: Dover Publications, Inc., 1956), Introduction, p. 18.

36 It should be pointed out, though, that this recycling is not inconsistent with there being a pattern of cosmic development and decline that eternally reiterates itself.

37 *Manuscript Remains*, Vol. I, Dresden, 1817, §662, p. 512.

38 Schopenhauer states in §54 and §63 that "Will" (rather than speaking more generally and referring to the "thing-in-itself") is "almighty," "absolutely free," and "entirely self-determining."

39 It was alluring to Friedrich Nietzsche, for example, who used the ideas in §54 as the basis of the theory of tragedy he developed in *The Birth of Tragedy* (1872), as well as of his conceptions of the superhuman (*der Übermensch*) and eternal recurrence.

40 The famous phrase occurs in Marx's introduction to the *A Contribution to the Critique of Hegel's Philosophy of Right* (1844), published coincidentally in the same year as the second edition of *The World as Will and Representation.*

41 It is perhaps natural to ask whether Schopenhauer had any children. Although he never married, he had two daughters during different times in his life—one was born in Dresden, in 1819; the other was born in Frankfurt, in 1835 or 1836—both of whom died very young.

42 Schopenhauer advocates a concept of "negative liberty," as articulated in a more contemporary form by Isaiah Berlin in his well-known essay, "Two Concepts of Liberty" (1958), published in his *Four Essays on Liberty* (Oxford: Oxford University Press, 1969).

43 Schopenhauer states near the end of §62 that (supposedly) according to Kant, "man dürfte den Menschen immer nur als Zweck, nie als Mittel behandeln."

44 Kant states in the second section of the *Foundations of the Metaphysics of Morals* (1785): "Handle so, daß du die Menschheit sowohl in deiner Person, als in der Person eines jeden andern jederzeit zugleich als Zweck, niemals bloß als Mittel brauchst."

45 See *Parerga and Paralipomena—Short Philosophical Essays*, Vol. II, trans. E. F. J. Payne (Oxford: Oxford University Press, 1974), chapter XII, "Additional Remarks on the Doctrine of the Suffering of the World," §149, p. 292.

46 The notebook excerpt is in *Manuscript Remains*, Vol. III, Reisebuch 1818–22, Section 98, p. 40, and the parallel excerpt in *The World as Will and Representation*, Vol. II, is in chapter XVIII, "On the Possibility of Knowing the Thing-in-Itself," Payne translation, pp. 196–198.

47 We find this interpretive line expressed in Moira Nicholls's essay "The Influences of Eastern Thought on Schopenhauer's Doctrine of the Thing-in-Itself," in Christopher Janaway, *The Cambridge Companion to Schopenhauer* (Cambridge: Cambridge University

NOTES

Press, 1989). John Atwell seems to say as much in his *Schopenhauer on the Character of the World: The Metaphysics of Will* (Berkeley/ Los Angeles/London: The University of California Press, 1995), chapter 5, as does Julian Young in his *Schopenhauer* (London and New York: Routledge, 2005), chapter four.

48 Schopenhauer's source is a work by Issak Jakob Schmidt (1779–1847), "On the Mahajana and Pradschna-Paramita." See I. J. Schmidt, *Über das Mahâjâna und Pradschnâ-Pâramita der Bauddhen, Mémoires de l'Académie Impériale des Sciences de St. Pétersbourg*, 6ᵗʰ Series, pt. 2 (Sciences Politiques, Histoire et Philologie), IV (1836), pp. 145–149.

49 Ludwig Wittgenstein, *Tractatus Logico-Philosophicus* [1921–22], in *Schriften*. Frankfurt am Main: Suhrkamp Verlag, 1060, p. 83 (translation by the author).

CHAPTER 4: RECEPTION AND INFLUENCE

1 After Wagner sent Schopenhauer a copy of his *Der Ring der Niebelungen*, Schopenhauer curtly responded that Wagner was greater as a poet than musician, that Wagner would be better off to stop writing music, and that Schopenhauer himself remained faithful to Rossini and Mozart. Arthur Hübscher, *The Philosophy of Schopenhauer in its Intellectual Context: Thinker Against the Tide*, trans. Joachim T. Baer and David E. Cartwright (Lewiston, NY: Edwin Mellen Press, 1989), p. 428.

2 *Beyond Good and Evil*, §36.

3 See, for example, *Beyond Good and Evil* (1886), §259, *The Birth of Tragedy*, "Attempt at Self-Criticism," §5 (1886), *On the Genealogy of Morals*, Second Essay, §11 (1887), and *The Antichrist*, §6 (1888).

4 Charles Youmans, "The Role of Nietzsche in Richard Strauss's Artistic Development." *Journal of Musicology*, Vol. 21, No. 3 (Summer 2004), pp. 309–342.

5 L. L. Whyte, *The Unconscious before Freud* (New York: Basic Books, 1960), p. 121.

6 Schopenhauer's chapter, "The Metaphysics of Sexual Love," that appears in the second edition of *The World as Will and Representation* (chapter XLIV) is most illuminating in this regard.

7 For a characterization of the Id, see Sigmund Freud, *New Introductory Lectures on Psychoanalysis* (1933), trans. James Strachey (New York: W. W. Norton & Company, 1965), pp. 65–66.

8 *New Introductory Lectures on Psychoanalysis*, p. 95.

9 Freud makes this explicit in his 1914 work, *The History of the Psychoanalytic Movement* (Kessinger Publishing, 2004), p. 7.

10 Nietzsche insightfully drew the connection between dreams and Platonic Ideas in *The Birth of Tragedy*, referring to them jointly as characterizing an "Apollonian" artistic register.

11 Neither Bahnsen's nor Mainländer's main works are available in English translation at present. For a summary of Bahnsen's views, see Harry Slochower, "Julius Bahnsen, Philosopher of Heroic Despair, 1830–1881," *The Philosophical Review*, Vol. 41, No. 4 (July 1932), pp. 368–384. Mainländer's main work is *Philosophie der Erlösung (Philosophy of Redemption)*, from 1876–77.

12 Borges states that, to him, the only philosophical view that seems to give an accurate semblance of the world is Schopenhauer's. See Jorge Luis Borges, *Other Inquisitions, 1937–1952*, trans. Ruth L. C. Simms (Austin: University of Texas Press, 1964), "Avatars of the Tortoise," p. 114.

13 Jorge Luis Borges, *Other Inquisitions, 1937–1952*, "The *Biathanatos*," p. 92.

14 Owen Knowles, "'Who's Afraid of Arthur Schopenhauer?': A New Context for Conrad's Heart of Darkness." *Nineteenth Century Literature*, Vol. 49, No. 1 (June 1994), pp. 75–106.

15 R. K. Gupta, "Moby Dick and Schopenhauer." *International Fiction Review*, 31.1–2 (2004), pp. 1–12.

16 Olive L. Fite, "Budd, Claggert and Schopenhauer." *Nineteenth-Century Fiction*, Vol. 23, No. 3 (December 1968), pp. 336–343.

17 T. J. Diffey, "Metaphysics and Aesthetics: A Case Study of Schopenhauer and Thomas Hardy," in Dale Jacquette (ed.), *Schopenhauer, Philosophy and the Arts* (Cambridge: Cambridge University Press, 1996), pp. 229–248.

18 Bryan Magee discusses Schopenhauer's influence on Hardy in his *The Philosophy of Schopenhauer* (Oxford: Oxford University Press, 1983), pp. 382–385. For an opposing opinion, see Robert Schweik's essay, "The Influence of Religion, Science and Philosophy on Hardy's Writings," in *The Cambridge Companion to Hardy* (Cambridge: Cambridge University Press, 1999), pp. 54–72.

19 Mitzi M. Bumsdale, "The Effect of Mrs. Rudolf Dircks' Translation of Schopenhauer's 'The Metaphysics of Love' on D. H. Lawrence." *Rocky Mountain Review of Language and Literature*, Vol. 32, No. 2 (Spring 1978), pp. 120–129.

20 Penelope LeFew-Blake, *Schopenhauer, Women's Literature, and the Legacy of Pessimism in the Novels of George Eliot, Olive Schreiner, Virginia Woolf and Doris Lessing* (Lewiston: The Edwin Mellen Press, 2001), p. 13. The synoptic essay, published without signature in *The Westminster Review*, was entitled "Iconoclasm in German Philosophy" (Vol. 59 [January and April, 1853], pp. 388–407). The author was John Oxenford.

21 This was completed by Tolstoy's friend, A. A. Fet, in 1881.

22 See Part Eight, chapter nine of *Anna Karenina*.

23 For an account of the relationship between Schopenhauer and symbolism, see "Schopenhauer According to the Symbolists: The Philosophical Roots of Late Nineteenth-Century Aesthetic Theory," by Shehira Doss-Davezac, in *Schopenhauer, Philosophy and the Arts*,

ed. Dale Jacquette (Cambridge: Cambridge University Press, 1996), pp. 249–276.

24 Joey Bonner, "The World as Will: Wang Kuo-wei and the Philosophy of Metaphysical Pessimism." *Philosophy East and West*, Vol. 29, No. 4 (1979), pp. 443–466.

25 Guy de Maupassant, "Beside a Dead Man" (1889), *The Works of Guy de Maupassant, Volume VIII* (Teddingdon, UK: The Echo Library, 2008), pp. 194–197.

26 Thomas Mann, "Schopenhauer" (1938) in *Essays by Thomas Mann* (New York: Vintage Books, 1957), p. 267.

27 Gottfried Büttner, "Schopenhauer's Recommendations to Beckett," *Samuel Beckett, Today/Aujourd'hui, Samuel Beckett: Endlessness in the Year 2000/Fin Sans Fin en l'an 2000, edited by/édité par Angela Moorjani and/et Carola Veit,* pp. 114–122 (9).

28 Emil Cioran, "Borges," in *Anathemas and Admirations* [1986–87] (London: Quartet Books, 1992), p. 225. Unlike Schopenhauer, though, Cioran (like Nietzsche) finds suffering to be revelatory rather than wholly repulsive.

29 *Machado de Assis*, by Earl E. Fitz (Boston: Twayne Publishers, 1989), p. 110. In connection with Machado's work in general, Fitz writes: "Like Thomas Hardy, with whom he can be legitimately compared, Machado de Assis shows how the forces of fate, of an indifferent universe, combine with the inconsistent and often contradictory aspects of human nature to undermine and destroy people" (p. 13).

30 For a chapter-length discussion of Schopenhauer's influence on Wittgenstein that develops this idea, see Robert Wicks, *Schopenhauer* (Oxford: Blackwell Publishing, 2008), pp. 173–183.

31 Peter Vergo, "Between Modernism and Tradition: The Importance of Klimt's Murals and Figure Paintings," in Colin B. Bailed (ed.), *Gustav Klimt. Modernism in the Making* (New York: Abrams; Ottawa: National Gallery of Canada, 2001), pp. 19–39.

32 Hans Frank, Governor-General of the occupied Polish territories during the Second World War, mentioned while he was in custody in Nuremberg, that Hitler carried with him copies of Homer and Schopenhauer during the War. See H. Frank, *Im Angesicht des Galgens* (Munich, 1953), p. 46.

33 For almost 30 years, Schopenhauer lived only a few minutes walking-distance from the Jewish ghetto in Frankfurt. In his writings, he contrasts Judaism with Christianity, Hinduism, and Buddhism, and from a theoretical standpoint condemns Judaism's optimism, in contrast to the three pessimistic religions he usually celebrates. Schopenhauer also has some highly critical remarks about "the Jewish view that regards the animal as something [merely] manufactured for man's use" (*Parerga and Paralipomena*, Vol. II, chapter XV, "On Religion," pp. 370–377).

34 The idea that art and beauty provide psychological relief is a common view, advocated by Freud as well. Another advocate is

Woody Allen—who was also influenced by Schopenhauer—insofar as he regards filmmaking as serving the important purpose of providing an oasis of delight, charm, and peace in the midst of the agony of human existence. See Robert E. Lauder, "Whatever Works: Woody Allen's World," *Commonweal*, April 15, 2010.

35 Manuel Terrazo, "Schopenhauer's Prolegomenon to Fuzziness," in *Fuzzy Optimization and Decision Making*, Vol. 3, Issue 3 (September 2004), pp. 227–254.

36 Bryan Magee, *The Philosophy of Schopenhauer* (Oxford: Oxford University Press, 1983), pp. 124–145.

NOTES FOR FURTHER READING

NOTES ON THE PRIMARY TEXT

A. Works by Schopenhauer, by original title and publication date

1813, *Über die vierfache Wurzel des Satzes vom zureichenden Grunde* (*On the Fourfold Root of the Principle of Sufficient Reason*)

1816, *Über das Sehn und die Farben* (*On Vision and Colors*)

1819 [1818], *Die Welt als Wille und Vorstellung* (*The World as Will and Representation*) [first edition, one volume]

1836, *Über den Willen in der Natur* (*On the Will in Nature*)

1839, "*Über die Freiheit des menschlichen Willens*" ("On Freedom of the Human Will")

1840, "*Über die Grundlage der Moral*" ("On the Basis of Morality")

1841 [1840], *Die beiden Grundprobleme der Ethik* (*The Two Fundamental Problems of Ethics*) [joint publication of the 1839 and 1840 essays in book form]

1844, *Die Welt als Wille und Vorstellung* (*The World as Will and Representation*) [second edition, two volumes]

1847, *Über die vierfache Wurzel des Satzes vom zureichenden Grunde* (*On the Fourfold Root of the Principle of Sufficient Reason*) [second edition, revised]

1851, *Parerga und Paralipomena*

1859, *Die Welt als Wille und Vorstellung* (*The World as Will and Representation*) [third edition, two volumes]

B. Full-length English translations of *Die Welt als Wille und Vorstellung*

1883: *The World as Will and Idea* (3 Vols.), trans. R. B. Haldane and J. Kemp. London: Routledge and Kegan Paul Ltd., 1883.

1958: *The World as Will and Representation*, Vols. I and II, trans. E. F. J. Payne [1958]. New York: Dover Publications, 1966.

2007: *The World as Will and Presentation*, Vol. I, trans. Richard Aquila in collaboration with David Carus. New York: Longman, 2007.

SECONDARY MATERIAL

A. Schopenhauer's Critiques of Kant

Guyer, Paul. "Schopenhauer, Kant, and the Methods of Philosophy," in *The Cambridge Companion to Schopenhauer*, ed. Christopher Janaway. Cambridge: Cambridge University Press, 1999, pp. 93–137.

Kelly, Michael. *Kant's Ethics and Schopenhauer's Criticism*. London: Swan Sonnenshein, 1910.

Tsanoff, R. A. *Schopenhauer's Criticism of Kant's Theory of Experience*. New York: Longmans, Green, 1911.

——. "Schopenhauer's Criticism of Kant's Theory of Ethics." *The Philosophical Review*, Vol. 19, No. 5 (September 1910), pp. 512–534.

Wicks, Robert. "Schopenhauer's Naturalization of Kant's *A Priori* Forms of Empirical Knowledge." *History of Philosophy Quarterly*, Vol. 10, No. 2 (April 1993), pp. 181–196.

Young, Julian. "Schopenhauer's Critique of Kantian Ethics." *Kant-Studien* 75 (1984), pp. 191–212.

B. *The Fourfold Root of the Principle of Sufficient Reason*

Griffiths, A. Phillips. "Wittgenstein and the Fourfold Root of the Principle of Sufficient Reason." *Proceedings of the Aristotelian Society*, Supplementary Volume L (1976), pp. 1–20.

Hamlyn, D. W. "Schopenhauer on the Principle of Sufficient Reason." *Royal Institute of Philosophy Lectures* (1971), 5: 145–162, Cambridge: Cambridge University Press.

Hamlyn, D. W. *Schopenhauer*. London: Routledge and Kegan Paul, 1980.

Jacquette, Dale. "Schopenhauer's Circle and the Principle of Sufficient Reason." *Metaphilosophy*, Vol. 23, No. 3 (1992), pp. 279–287.

White, F. C. *On Schopenhauer's Fourfold Root of the Principle of Sufficient Reason*. Leiden: E.J. Brill, 1992.

——. "The Fourfold Root," in Christopher Janaway (ed.), *The Cambridge Companion to Schopenhauer*. Cambridge: Cambridge University Press, 1999, pp. 63–92.

White, F. C. (ed.). *Schopenhauer's Early Fourfold Root: Translation and Commentary*. Aldershot: Avebury, Ashgate Publishing, Ltd, 1997.

C. Schopenhauer and Will

Atwell, J. *Schopenhauer on the Character of the World*. Berkeley: University of California Press, 1995.

Copleston, F. *Arthur Schopenhauer: Philosopher of Pessimism* [1946]. London: Barnes and Noble, 1975.

Gardiner, Patrick. *Schopenhauer*. Middlesex: Penguin Books, 1967.

Jacquette, Dale. *The Philosophy of Schopenhauer*. Chesham, UK: Acumen, 2005.

Janaway, Christopher. *Schopenhauer*. Oxford: Oxford University Press, 1994.

——. *Self and World in Schopenhauer's Philosophy*. Oxford: Clarendon Press, 1989.

Magee, Bryan. *The Philosophy of Schopenhauer*. Oxford: Clarendon Press, 1983.

Neeley, S. G. *Schopenhauer: A Consistent Reading.* Lewiston, NY: Edwin Mellen Press, 2004.

Soll, Ivan. "On Desire and its Discontents." *Ratio: An International Journal of Analytic Philosophy,* Vol. 2, No. 2 (December 1989), pp. 159–184.

Wicks, Robert. *Schopenhauer.* Oxford: Blackwell Publishing, 2008.

Young, J. *Schopenhauer.* London and New York: Routledge, 2005.

—. *Willing and Unwilling: A Study in the Philosophy of Arthur Schopenhauer.* Dordrecht: Martinus Nijhoff, 1987.

D. Schopenhauer and Art/Music/Aesthetics/Platonic Ideas

Alperson, Philip. "Schopenhauer's Account of Aesthetic Experience." *The British Journal of Aesthetics*, Vol. 30, No. 2 (1990), pp. 132–142.

—. "Schopenhauer and Musical Revelation." *The Journal of Aesthetics and Art Criticism*, Vol. 40, No. 2 (Winter 1981), pp. 155–166.

Chansky, James D. "Schopenhauer and Platonic Ideas: A Groundwork for an Aesthetic Metaphysic," in Luft, Eric von der (ed.), *Schopenhauer: New Essays in Honor of His 200th Birthday.* Lewiston, NY: Edwin Mellen Press, 1988, pp. 67–81.

Gupta, R. K. "Schopenhauer on Literature and Art." *Schopenhauer-Jahrbuch*, 62 (1981), pp. 156–168.

Hall, Robert W. "Schopenhauer: Music and the Emotions." *Schopenhauer-Jahrbuch*, 83 (2002), pp. 151–161.

Hein, Hilde. "Schopenhauer and Platonic Ideas." *Journal of the History of Philosophy*, Vol. 4, No. 2 (1966), pp. 133–144.

Jacquette, D. (ed.). *Schopenhauer, Philosophy and the Arts.* Cambridge: Cambridge University Press, 1996 (contains 13 essays).

Jacquette, Dale. "Schopenhauer on the Antipathy of Aesthetic Genius and the Charming." *History of European Ideas*, Vol. 18, No. 3 (May 1994), pp. 373–385.

Knox, Israel. "Schopenhauer's Aesthetic Theory," in Michael Fox (ed.), *Schopenhauer: His Philosophical Achievement.* Sussex: The Harvester Press; Totowa NJ: Barnes & Noble Books, 1980, pp. 132–146.

Krueger, Steven. "Schopenhauer on the Pleasures of Tragedy." *Schopenhauer-Jahrbuch,* 82 (2001), pp. 113–120.

Neeley, G. Steven. "Schopenhauer and the Platonic Ideas: A Reconsideration." *Idealistic Studies*, Vol. 30, No. 2 (Spring–Summer 2000), pp. 121–148.

Neill, Alex and Christopher Janaway (eds.). *Better Consciousness: Schopenhauer's Philosophy of Value.* London: Wiley-Blackwell, 2009.

Neureiter, Paul R. "Schopenhauer's Will as Aesthetic Criterion." *Journal of Value Inquiry*, Vol. 20 (1986), pp. 41–50.

Taylor, Terri Graves. "Platonic Ideas, Aesthetic Experience, and the Resolution of Schopenhauer's Great Contradiction." *International Studies in Philosophy*, Vol. 19, No. 3 (1987), pp. 43–53.

Trigg, Dylan. "Schopenhauer and the Sublime Pleasure of Tragedy." *Philosophy and Literature*, Vol. 28, No. 1 (April 2004), pp. 165–179.

Vandenabeele, Bart. "On the Notion of 'Disinterestedness': Kant, Lyotard, and Schopenhauer." *Journal of the History of Ideas*, Vol. 62, No. 4 (October 2001), pp. 705–720.

——. "Schopenhauer on the Beautiful and the Sublime: A Qualitative or Gradual Distinction?" *Schopenhauer-Jahrbuch*, 82 (2001), pp. 99–112.

White, Pamela. "Schopenhauer and Schoenberg." *Journal of the Arnold Schoenberg Institute*, Vol. 8, No. 1 (1984), pp. 39–57.

Young, Julian P. "The Standpoint of Eternity: Schopenhauer on Art." *Kant-Studien*, 78 (1987), pp. 424–441.

E. Schopenhauer and morality

Atwell, John. *Schopenhauer: The Human Character.* Philadelphia: Temple University Press, 1990.

Berger, Douglas L. "Does Monism do Ethical Work?: Assessing Hacker's Critique of Vedāntic and Schopenhauerian Ethics." *Schopenhauer-Jahrbuch*, 88 (2007), pp. 29–37.

Cartwright, David E. "Compassion and Solidarity with Sufferers: The Metaphysics of Mitleid," in Alex Neill and Christopher Janaway (eds.), *Better Consciousness: Schopenhauer's Philosophy of Value.* London: Wiley-Blackwell, 2009.

——. "Kant, Schopenhauer, and Nietzsche on the Morality of Pity." *Journal of the History of Ideas*, Vol. 45, No. 1 (January–March, 1984), pp. 83–98.

——. "Schopenhauer as Moral Philosopher—Towards the Actuality of His Ethics." *Schopenhauer-Jahrbuch*, 70 (1989), pp. 54–65.

——. "Schopenhauer's Axiological Analysis of Character." *Revue Internationale de Philosophie,* 42 (1988), pp. 18–36.

——. "Schopenhauer's Compassion and Nietzsche's Pity." *Schopenhauer-Jahrbuch*, 69 (1988), pp. 557–567.

——. "Schopenhauer's Narrower Sense of Morality," in Christopher Janaway (ed.), *The Cambridge Companion to Schopenhauer.* Cambridge: Cambridge University Press, 1999, pp. 252–292.

Goodman, R. B. "Schopenhauer and Wittgenstein on Ethics." *Journal of the History of Philosophy,* Vol. 17, No. 4 (1979), pp. 437–447.

Griffiths, P. "Wittgenstein, Schopenhauer and Ethics," in G. Vesey (ed.), *Understanding Wittgenstein.* London: Macmillan, 1974, pp. 96–116.

Lauxtermann, P. F. H. *Schopenhauer's Broken World View: Colours and Ethics Between Kant and Goethe.* Dordrecht: Kluwer Academic Publishers, 2000.

Maidan, Michael. "Schopenhauer on Altruism and Morality." *Schopenhauer-Jahrbuch*, 69 (1988), pp. 265–272.

Mannion, Gerald. *Schopenhauer, Religion and Morality: The Humble Path to Ethics.* Burlington, VT: Ashgate Publishing Company, 2003.

Marcin, R. B. *In Search of Schopenhauer's Cat: Arthur Schopenhauer's Quantum-mystical Theory of Justice.* Washington, D.C.: The Catholic University of America Press, 2006.

Nicholls, Roderick. "Schopenhauer's Analysis of Character," in Michael Fox (ed.), *Schopenhauer: His Philosophical Achievement*. Sussex: The Harvester Press; Totowa NJ: Barnes & Noble Books, 1980, pp. 107–131.

Taylor, Richard. "On the Basis of Morality," in Michael Fox (ed.), *Schopenhauer: His Philosophical Achievement*. Sussex: The Harvester Press; Totowa NJ: Barnes & Noble Books, 1980, pp. 95–106.

F. Schopenhauer and Asian Philosophy

Abelsen, Peter. "Schopenhauer and Buddhism." *Philosophy East & West*, 43, 2 (1993), pp. 255–278.

App, Urs. "Schopenhauer's Initial Encounter with Indian Thought." *Schopenhauer-Jahrbuch*, 87 (2006), pp. 35–76.

Barua, Arati (ed.). *Schopenhauer and Indian Philosophy*. New Delhi: Northern Book Centre, 2008.

Berger, D. L. *The Veil of Maya: Schopenhauer's System and Early Indian Thought*. Binghamton, NY: Global Academic Publishing, 2004.

Bonner, Joey. "The World as Will: Wang Kuo-Wei and the Philosophy of Metaphysical Pessimism." *Philosophy East and West*, Vol. 29, No. 4 (October, 1979), pp. 443–466.

—. *Wang Kuo-wei: An Intellectual Biography*. Cambridge, MA: Harvard University Press, 1986.

Dauer, Dorothea W. *Schopenhauer as Transmitter of Buddhist Ideas*, European University Papers, Series 1, Vol. 15. Berne: Herbert Lang, 1969.

Dharmasiri, Gunapala. "Principles and Justification in Morals: The Buddha and Schopenhauer." *Schopenhauer-Jahrbuch*, 53 (1972), pp. 88–92.

Kishan, B. V. "Schopenhauer and Buddhism," in Michael Fox (ed.), *Schopenhauer: His Philosophical Achievement*. Sussex: Harvester Press, 1980, pp. 255–261.

Nanajivako, Bhikkhu. *Schopenhauer and Buddhism*. Sri Lanka: Buddhist Publication Society, 1970.

Nicholls, Moira. "The Influences of Eastern Thought on Schopenhauer's Doctrine of the Thing-in-Itself," in Christopher Janaway (ed.), *The Cambridge Companion to Schopenhauer*. Cambridge: Cambridge University Press, 1999, pp. 171–212.

Pandey, Kanti Chandra. "Svatantryavada of Kashmir and Voluntarism of Schopenhauer." *Schopenhauer-Jahrbuch*, 48 (1967), pp. 159–167.

Sedlar, Jean W. *India in the Mind of Germany: Schelling, Schopenhauer, and Their Times*. Lanham, MD: University Press of America, 1982.

Vukomanović, Milan. "Schopenhauer and Wittgenstein: Assessing the Buddhist Influences on Their Conceptions of Ethics." *Filozofija i društvo*, XXIV (2004), pp. 163–187.

G. Schopenhauer and Nietzsche

(See also the section on Schopenhauer and Morality above.)

Copleston, Frederick. "Schopenhauer and Nietzsche," in Michael Fox (ed.), *Schopenhauer: His Philosophical Achievement*. Sussex: The Harvester Press; Totowa NJ: Barnes & Noble Books, 1980, pp. 215–225.

Dolson, Grace Neal. "The Influence of Schopenhauer upon Friedrich Nietzsche." *Philosophical Review*, 10 (1901), pp. 241–250.

Janaway, Christopher. "Nietzsche, the Self and Schopenhauer," in Keith Ansell-Pearson (ed.), *Nietzsche and Modern German Thought*. London: Routledge, 1991, pp. 119–142.

—. (ed.). *Willing and Nothingness: Schopenhauer as Nietzsche's Educator*. Oxford: Clarendon Press, 1998.

Ray, Matthew Alun. "Subjectivity and Irreligion: Atheism and Agnosticism in Kant, Schopenhauer and Nietzsche.". *Review of Metaphysics*, Vol. 59, No. 1 (2005), pp. 194–196.

Santayana, George. "Schopenhauer and Nietzsche," in *The German Mind: A Philosophical Diagnosis*. New York: Thomas Y. Crowell, 1968, pp. 114–122.

Schweitzer, Albert. "Schopenhauer and Nietzsche," in *Civilization and Ethics* (*The Philosophy of Civilization*, Part II), trans. C. T. Campion, 2nd edition. London: A. & C. Black, 1929, pp. 165–180.

Simmel, Georg. *Schopenhauer and Nietzsche* [1907], trans. Helmut Loiskandl, Deena Weinstein, and Michael Weinstein. Amherst: University of Massachusetts Press, 1986.

Taminiaux, Jacques. "Art and Truth in Schopenhauer and Nietzsche." *Man and World*, Vol. 20, No. 1 (March 1987), pp. 85–102.

Touey, Daniel. "Schopenhauer and Nietzsche on the Nature and Limits of Philosophy." *The Journal of Value Inquiry*, Vol. 32, No. 2 (June 1998), pp. 243–252.

Ure, Michael. "The Irony of Pity: Nietzsche contra Schopenhauer and Rousseau." *Journal of Nietzsche Studies*, Issue 32 (2006), pp. 68–91.

Vandenabeele, Bart. "Schopenhauer, Nietzsche and the Aesthetically Sublime." *Journal of Aesthetic Education*, Vol. 37, No. 1 (Spring 2003), pp. 90–106.

Wicks, Robert. "Schopenhauerian Moral Awareness as a Source of Nietzschean Non-Morality." *Journal of Nietzsche Studies*, Issue 23 (2002), pp. 21–38.

Young, Julian. "Immaculate Perception: Nietzsche contra Schopenhauer." *Schopenhauer-Jahrbuch*, 74 (1993), pp. 73–85.

H. Schopenhauer and German Idealism (Fichte, Schelling, Hegel)

Angus, Ian. "A Historical Entry into the Problem of Time: Hegel and Schopenhauer." *Kinesis: Graduate Journal in Philosophy*, Vol. 6 (Fall, 1974), pp. 3–14.

Ausmus, Harry J. "Schopenhauer's View of History: A Note." *History and Theory: Studies in the Philosophy of History*, Vol. 15 (1976), pp. 141–145.

Chansky, James. "The Conscious Body: Schopenhauer's Difference from Fichte in Relation to Kant." *International Studies in Philosophy*, Vol. 24, No. 3 (1992), pp. 25–44.

Gottfried, Paul. "Arthur Schopenhauer as a Critic of History." *Journal of the History of Ideas*, Vol. 36 (April–June, 1975), pp. 331–338.

Korab-Karpowicz, W. J. "A Point of Reconciliation Between Schopenhauer and Hegel." *Owl of Minerva*, Vol. 21, No. 2 (Spring, 1990), pp. 167–175.

Lauxtermann, P. F. H. "Hegel and Schopenhauer as Partisans of Goethe's Theory of Color." *Journal of the History of Ideas*, Vol. 51, No. 4 (October–December, 1990), pp. 599–624.

Soll, Ivan. "On Desire and its Discontents." *Ratio: An International Journal of Analytic Philosophy*, Vol. 2, No. 2 (December 1989), pp. 159–184.

Wicks, Robert. *Schopenhauer*. Blackwell, 2008, chapter 12, "Schopenhauer, Hegel and Alienated Labor," pp. 161–172.

I. Edited general collections

Fox, M. (ed.). *Schopenhauer: His Philosophical Achievement*. Brighton: Harvester Press, 1980.

Janaway, Christopher. *The Cambridge Companion to Schopenhauer*. Cambridge: Cambridge University Press, 1999.

Luft, Eric von der (ed.). *Schopenhauer: New Essays in Honor of His 200th Birthday*. Lewiston, NY: Edwin Mellen Press, 1988.

Vandenabeele, Bart (ed.). *Companion to Schopenhauer* (Blackwell Companions to Philosophy Series). Oxford: Wiley-Blackwell, 2011.

J. Biographies of Schopenhauer in English

Bridgewater, P. *Arthur Schopenhauer's English Schooling*. London and New York: Routledge, 1988.

Cartwright, David E. *Schopenhauer: A Biography*. Cambridge: Cambridge University Press, 2010.

McGill, V. J. *Schopenhauer: Pessimist and Pagan* [1931]. New York: Haskell House Publishers, Ltd., 1971.

Safranski, R. *Schopenhauer and the Wild Years of Philosophy*, trans. Ewald Osers. London: Weidenfeld and Nicholson, 1989.

Wallace, William. *Life of Arthur Schopenhauer*. London: Walter Scott, 1890.

Zimmern, Helen. *Arthur Schopenhauer: His Life and Philosophy*. London: Longmans Green & Co., 1876.

SELECTIVE BIBLIOGRAPHY

Aristotle. *Poetics*, trans. Richard Janko. Indianapolis/Cambridge: Hackett Publishing Company, 1987.

Atwell, J. *Schopenhauer on the Character of the World*. Berkeley: University of California Press, 1995.

Augustine. *The Confessions of Saint Augustine*, trans. Edward B. Pusey, D. D. New York: Washington Square Press, 1951.

Berkeley, George. *The Principles of Human Knowledge* [1710], ed. Colin Murray Turbane. Indianapolis/New York: The Bobbs-Merrill Company, Inc., 1970.

Berlin, Isaiah. "Two Concepts of Liberty" (1958), published in his *Four Essays on Liberty*. Oxford: Oxford University Press, 1969.

Bonner, Joey. "The World as Will: Wang Kuo-Wei and the Philosophy of Metaphysical Pessimism." *Philosophy East and West*, Vol. 29, No. 4 (October, 1979), pp. 443–466.

Borges, Jorge Luis. *Other Inquisitions, 1937–1952*, trans. Ruth L. C. Simms. Austin: University of Texas Press, 1964.

Burnsdale, Mitzi. "The Effect of Mrs. Rudolf Dircks' Translation of Schopenhauer's 'The Metaphysics of Love' on D. H. Lawrence." *Rocky Mountain Review of Language and Literature*, Vol. 32, No. 2 (Spring 1978).

Büttner, Gottfried. "Schopenhauer's Recommendations to Beckett," *Samuel Beckett, Today/Aujourd'hui, Samuel Beckett: Endlessness in the Year 2000/Fin Sans Fin en l'an 2000, edited by/édité par Angela Moorjani and/et Carola Veit, (9)*.

Cioran, E. M. "Borges." *Anathemas and Admirations* [1986–87]. London: Quartet Books, 1992.

Doss-Davezac, Shehira. "Schopenhauer According to the Symbolists: The Philosophical Roots of Late Nineteenth-Century Aesthetic Theory." *Schopenhauer, Philosophy and the Arts*, ed. Dale Jacquette. Cambridge: Cambridge University Press, 1996.

Fite, Olive L. "Budd, Claggert and Schopenhauer." *Nineteenth-Century Fiction*, Vol. 23, No. 3 (December 1968), pp. 336–343.

Fitz, Earl E. *Machado de Assis*. Boston: Twayne Publishers, 1989.

Frank, H. *Im Angesicht des Galgens*. München-Gräfelfing, Munich: Friedrich Alfred Beck Verlag, 1953.

Freud, Sigmund. *New Introductory Lectures on Psychoanalysis* (1933), trans. James Strachey. New York: W. W. Norton & Company, 1965.

—. *The History of the Psychoanalytic Movement* [1914]. Whitefish, MT: Kessinger Publishing, 2004.

Gardiner, Patrick. *Schopenhauer*. Harmondsworth, UK: Penguin Books, 1967.

Gupta, R. K. "Moby Dick and Schopenhauer." *International Fiction Review*, 31.1–2 (2004), pp. 1–12.

Hegel, G. W. F. *The Philosophy of History*. New York: Dover Publications, Inc., 1956.

Herrigel, Eugen. *Zen in the Art of Archery* [1948], trans. R. F. C. Hull. New York: Vintage Books, 1971.

Hofstadter, Douglas R. *Gödel, Escher, Bach: An Eternal Golden Braid*. New York: Vintage Books, 1980.

Hübscher, Arthur. *The Philosophy of Schopenhauer in its Intellectual Context: Thinker Against the Tide*, trans. Joachim T. Baer and David E. Cartwright. Lewiston, NY: Edwin Mellen Press, 1989.

Kant, Immanuel. *Critique of the Power of Judgment*, trans. Paul Guyer and Eric Matthews. Cambridge: Cambridge University Press, 2000.

Knowles, Owen. "'Who's Afraid of Arthur Schopenhauer?': A New Context for Conrad's Heart of Darkness." *Nineteenth Century Literature*, Vol. 49, No. 1 (June 1994).

LeFew-Blake, Penelope. *Schopenhauer, Women's Literature, and the Legacy of Pessimism in the Novels of George Eliot, Olive Schreiner, Virginia Woolf and Doris Lessing*. Lewiston: The Edwin Mellen Press, 2001.

Lewis, Peter B. "Schopenhauer's Laughter." *The Monist*, Vol. 88, No. 1 (2005).

Locke, John. *An Essay Concerning Human Understanding*. London: Thomas Tegg, 1841.

Magee, Bryan. *The Philosophy of Schopenhauer*. Oxford: Oxford University Press, 1983.

Mainländer, Philipp. *Philosophie der Erlösung* (1879). Whitefish, MT: Kessinger Publishing, 2009.

Mann, Thomas. "Schopenhauer" (1938). *Essays by Thomas Mann*. New York: Vintage Books, 1957.

Maupassant, Guy de. "Beside a Dead Man" (1889), *The Works of Guy de Maupassant, Volume VIII*. Teddingdon, UK: The Echo Library, 2008.

Mc Taggert, John Ellis. "The Unreality of Time." *Mind: A Quarterly Review of Psychology and Philosophy*, 17 (1908), pp. 456–473.

Nicholls, Moira. "The Influences of Eastern Thought on Schopenhauer's Doctrine of the Thing-in-Itself," in Christopher Janaway (ed.), *The Cambridge Companion to Schopenhauer*. Cambridge: Cambridge University Press, 1999.

Nietzsche, Friedrich. *Beyond Good and Evil*, trans. Walter Kaufmann. New York: Vintage Books, 1966.

—. *On the Genealogy of Morals*, trans. Walter Kaufmann. New York: Vintage Books, 1969.

—. *The Antichrist*, in *The Portable Nietzsche*, trans. Walter Kaufmann. New York: The Viking Press, 1954.

—. *The Birth of Tragedy*, trans. Walter Kaufmann. New York: Vintage Books, 1967.

Schmidt, I. J. *Über das Mahâjâna und Pradschnâ-Pâramita der Bauddhen, Mémoires de l'Académie Impériale des Sciences de St. Pétersbourg*, 6th Series, pt. 2 (Sciences Politiques, Histoire et Philologie), IV (1836), pp. 145–149.

Schopenhauer, Arthur. *Essay on the Freedom of the Will*, trans. Konstantin Kolenda. Indianapolis and New York: The Bobbs-Merrill Company, Inc., 1960.

—. *The Fourfold Root of the Principle of Sufficient Reason*, trans. E. F. J. Payne. LaSalle, Ill: Open Court Publishing Company, 1974.

—. *Manuscript Remains in Four Volumes*, ed. Arthur Hübscher, trans. E. F. J. Payne. Oxford, New York, Munich: Berg, 1988.

—. *On the Basis of Morality*, trans. E. F. J. Payne. Indianapolis and New York: The Bobbs-Merrill Company, Inc., 1965.

—. *On the Fourfold Root of the Principle of Sufficient Reason and On the Will in Nature: Two Essays by Schopenhauer*, trans. Mme. Karl Hillebrand. London: George Bell and Sons, 1891.

—. *Parerga and Paralipomena: Short Philosophical Essays*, trans. E. F. J. Payne, Vols. I and II. Oxford: Clarendon Press, 1974.

—. *The World as Will and Idea*, (3 Vols.), trans. R. B. Haldane and J. Kemp. London: Routledge and Kegan Paul Ltd., 1883.

—. *The World as Will and Representation*, Vols. I and II, trans. E. F. J. Payne. New York: Dover Publications, 1966.

Schweik, Robert. "The Influence of Religion, Science and Philosophy on Hardy's Writings," in *The Cambridge Companion to Hardy*. Cambridge: Cambridge University Press, 1999.

Slochower, Harry. "Julius Bahnsen, Philosopher of Heroic Despair, 1830–1881." *The Philosophical Review*, Vol. 41, No. 4 (July 1932).

Stendhal (Maris-Henri Beyle), *De l'amour* [1822]. Paris: Gallimard, 1969.

Tarrazo, Manuel. "Schopenhauer's Prolegomenon to Fuzziness." *Fuzzy Optimization and Decision Making*, Vol. 3, Issue 3 (September 2004).

Vergo, Peter. "Between Modernism and Tradition: The Importance of Klimt's Murals and Figure Paintings." *Gustav Klimt. Modernism in the Making*, Colin B. Bailed (ed.). New York: Abrams; Ottawa: National Gallery of Canada, 2001.

Whyte, L. L. *The Unconscious before Freud*. New York: Basic Books, 1960.

Wicks, Robert. *Schopenhauer*. Oxford: Blackwell Publishing, 2008.

Youmans, Charles. "The Role of Nietzsche in Richard Strauss's Artistic Development." *Journal of Musicology*, Vol. 21, No. 3 (Summer 2004), pp. 309–342.

Young, Julian. *Schopenhauer*. London and New York: Routledge, 2005.

INDEX

abstract concepts
    see representations
abstract ideas *see* representations
acquired character *see* character
Adam 122, 141
Adler, George J. 155
aesthetic experience *see* Platonic
    Idea(s)
affirmation of the will-to-live
    see Will
Allen, Woody 167
"all life is suffering" 118
animal magnetism 161
architecture 15, 100
argument from analogy 63–4
Aristotle 31, 46, 98, 106, 111
art
    as the communication of
        Platonic Ideas 15, 92, 156
    see also beauty; genius;
        Platonic Idea(s);
        architecture, sculpture,
        painting, music, poetry
asceticism 16, 23, 110, 136, 137,
    140, 142, 145, 161 *see also*
    Will: denial-of-the-Will
Atwell, John 164
Augustine 71, 141, 159

badness (of character)
    see character
Bahnsen, Julius 154
beauty
    as the apprehension of ideal
        types *see* Platonic Idea(s)
    emerges through conflict 77
    inconsistent with sexual
        allure 97

    involves a feeling of
        timelessness 86
    natural beauty as
        deceptive 153
    as the promise of happiness
        (Stendhal) 97
    provides metaphysical
        insight 85
    two dimensions of 99
Beckett, Samuel 156
Beethoven, Ludwig van 148
bellum omnium contra omnes
    124, 151
Berkeley, George 34, 67–8,
    159–60
boredom 97, 109, 118, 119
Borges, Jorge Luis 154, 156
Buddhism 17, 23, 110, 129,
    143–6, 166
    Buddha 2, 5, 104
    Diamond Sutra 146
    nirvana 129, 145
    Prajñāpāramitā 145–6
    Zen Buddhism 47, 146
bulldog-ant of Australia 76

Calderón 6
causality 11–13, 27–9, 31, 32,
    36–43, 52, 55, 56, 61, 69, 83,
    87, 91, 93, 108
character
    acquired character 116
    the "bad" person 9, 16,
        130, 131, 133, 135, 137,
        139, 161
    empirical character 66, 140
    the "good" person 132–4,
        155